Virginia Woolf

Titles in the series Critical Lives present the work of leading cultural figures of the modern period. Each book explores the life of the artist, writer, philosopher or architect in question and relates it to their major works.

In the same series

Virginia Woolf

Ira Nadel

REAKTION BOOKS

For Anne

Published by Reaktion Books Ltd
Unit 32, Waterside
44–48 Wharf Road
London N1 7UX, UK
www.reaktionbooks.co.uk

First published 2016

Printed and bound in Great Britain by Bell & Bain, Glasgow

A catalogue record for this book is available from the British Library

ISBN 978 1 78023 666 7

Contents

Abbreviations

BA   *Between the Acts* [1941], ed. Frank Kermode (Oxford, 2008)

D   *The Diary of Virginia Woolf*, ed. Anne Olivier Bell, assisted by Andrew McNeillie, 5 vols (San Diego, CA, 1977–84)

JR   *Jacob's Room* [1922], ed. Kate Flint (Oxford, 2008)

LETT *The Letters of Virginia Woolf*, ed. Nigel Nicolson and Joanne Trautmann, 6 vols (San Diego, CA, 1975–80)

MD   *Mrs Dalloway* [1925], ed. David Bradshaw, new edn (Oxford, 2000)

OR   *Orlando* [1928], ed. Rachel Bowlby (Oxford, 2008)

RM   *A Room of One's Own* [1929] (Peterborough, ON, 2001)

TL   *To the Lighthouse* [1927], ed. David Bradshaw (Oxford, 2006)

VO   *The Voyage Out* [1915], ed. Lorna Sage (Oxford, 2009)

W   *The Waves* [1931], ed. Gillian Beer (Oxford, 2008)

Y   *The Years* [1937], ed. Hermione Lee (Oxford, 2009)

Introduction

To be flung into the sea . . . the idea was incoherently delightful.

Virginia Woolf, *The Voyage Out*

With Leonard Woolf at her side, the thirty-year-old Virginia
Stephen attended the board of inquiry into the sinking of the
Titanic held at the London Scottish Drill Hall, at 59 Buckingham
Gate, not far from Buckingham Palace, on the first day of witness
testimony, 3 May 1912. The two of them entered a capacious,
glass-roofed, sunlit hall modelled like a courtroom: rows of seats
faced the dais where Lord Mersey and his assessors sat in front
of a maroon curtain. Poor acoustics, however, muffled answers,
requiring sounding boards to be placed before the assessors and
any witnesses. A 6-metre (20-foot) model of the *Titanic* and an
immense map of the North Atlantic stood behind the witness
stand. The press filled the front rows, the remaining space and the
galleries on the side for spectators. The first witness was the ship's
lookout, Archie Jewell, who detailed the routines of his job. The
second was Joseph Scarrott, an able-bodied seaman who took
charge of Lifeboat 14 and who offered a graphic description of
the sinking and the events immediately following.

The week before they attended, Leonard had resigned from his
Civil Service appointment in Ceylon to remain in England to pursue
Virginia Stephen; he had asked her to marry him in January but
she had not yet accepted. She still had doubts. Virginia – hereafter

Woolf – was eager to attend the *Titanic* hearings and although they sat through only one day of what would be 36 days of testimony from 97 witnesses, she followed the inquiry in the press and the statements by Lady Duff-Gordon and Sir Cosmos (who supposedly bought his way into Lifeboat 1), Bruce Ismay, managing director of White Star Lines, and Sir Ernest Shackleton, Antarctic explorer. The final report was published on 30 July 1912. Woolf was alert to the facts and the loss of life.

The catastrophe captivated the young Virginia Woolf, who became absorbed with the disaster, writing to a friend in April 1912, shortly after the sinking but before the inquiry, that she wanted to write a full account of the wreck, adding an odd detail in her letter that at that depth ships do not sink 'but remain poised half way down, and become perfectly flat' (*LETT*, 1, 495). The image of the suspended ship (clearly an imagined contrast to the wreck on the seabed) represents the uneasy balance of Woolf's mental and creative life, and the essential repression of traumatic events in her past, which unexpectedly surface to create her mental instability but also her creative energy. Not surprisingly, her first novel, *The Voyage Out*, is about a sea voyage and ends with the death of the heroine, who has a vision of drowning; Virginia Woolf drowned, by suicide, on 28 March 1941.

Water is a persistent trope for Woolf, appearing and reappearing constantly in both her life and writing to such a degree that she could not separate one from the other. In her reminiscence of her childhood and sister Vanessa, she writes that 'we drifted together like ships in an immense ocean'.[1] Earlier, in 1899, she wrote a semi-comic account of a rowing boat overturning with herself and two others on board and the fear of her family that she had drowned. Entitled 'A Terrible Tragedy in a Duckpond' and written in the style of a newspaper report, plus an addendum composed in 1904 by one of the supposedly drowned children, it contains a vivid description of near drowning.[2] In her letters, Woolf links the world of water to her mental state, writing to Vita Sackville-West in 1926 that 'I haven't said anything very much, or given you any notion of the terrific high waves, and the infernal deep gulfs, on which I mount and toss in a few days' (*LETT*, III, 237). In *To the Lighthouse*, Prue observes that 'one can hardly tell which is the sea and which is the land' (*TL*, 103). Two years after the novel appeared, Woolf wrote in her diary: 'I shall pass like a cloud on the waves' (*D*, III, 218). Crossing Trafalgar Square one day, she records that she was held up by the singing and dancing of a choir celebrating Lifeboat Day. On Christmas Day 1922, Woolf wrote to the young writer Gerald Brenan, offering the following self-criticism and wondering

> why it is that though I try sometimes to limit myself . . .
> to the things I do well, I am always drawn on and on, by
> human beings, I think, out of the little circle of safety, on
> and on, to the whirlpools; when I go under.' (*LETT*, II, 600)

This fear of going under is what drove Woolf to write and yet caused her anxiety about living.

Woolf's life was a voyaging out from the late Edwardian existence of Hyde Park Gate to, first, the modern but uncharted world of Bloomsbury, and then further outwards to Hogarth House in Richmond and Monk's House in Sussex. But at each stage she remained uneasily suspended below the surface, echoing her thoughts on the *Titanic*, which according to one critic 'brought to culmination the imagery of the Abyss in the late Victorian and Edwardian periods'.[3] The backdrop is Woolf's continual mental instability, which she outlined to Leonard two days before they attended the *Titanic* inquiry. On 1 May 1912 she told him: 'I pass from hot to cold in an instant, without any reason; except that I believe sheer physical effort and exhaustion influence me' (*LETT*, I, 496). But she also realized, as she wrote in her essay 'How Should

One Read a Book?', that 'we learn through feeling; we cannot suppress our own idiosyncrasy without impoverishing it.'[4]

How to read Virginia Woolf's life, as well as her work, is the aim of this 'Critical Life', which will examine the formative elements of her personal and authorial identity as she moved from the enclosed space of Hyde Park Gate to the open and free-spirited Bloomsbury of Gordon Square and then from the inventive world of Hogarth House and the Hogarth Press to the alternating refuge and anxiety of Monk's House. Her concern with history, narrative, art and friendship – plus the experimental nature of her fiction – will be of critical interest.

Each chapter will begin by introducing a place, followed by one or two themes that connect that stage and location of her life with her work. As Woolf would later write in an essay on the homes of Keats and Carlyle, 'we know them from their houses.' Artists, she added, stamp themselves on their space; they have a 'faculty . . . for making the table, the chair, the curtain, the carpet into their own image'.[5]

Family and memory will inaugurate the narrative but among the critical questions addressed throughout will be the origin of Woolf's breakdowns (four between the ages of thirteen and 33, with a fifth imminent at age 59), her attitude towards sex, her uncertain social and political views (a radical? a socialist? a snob? a commoner?), the nature of her marriage to Leonard Woolf, her relationship with Vita Sackville-West and the toll of writing upon her state of mind. She never finished a work with satisfaction, but with anxiety and worry, often thinking of herself as a failure. A further consideration will be her technique as a novelist and the skills she learned from reading the works of others, as in this passage derived from reading Turgenev:

> If we want to describe a summer evening, the way to do it
> is to set people talking in a room with their backs to the

Virginia Stephen in July 1902, photograph by George Charles Beresford.

window, and then, as they talk about something else, let someone half turn her head and say, 'a fine evening'.[6]

The situation in *The Voyage Out*, composed two years after the sinking of the *Titanic*, narrates Rachel Vinrace's journey from England to South America. The heroine embarks on a journey out, and does not return. With an implicit allusion to the tragic fate of the great ship of the White Star Line, Richard tells Rachel in the novel 'what solitary icebergs we are . . . How little we can communicate' (*vo*, 79). Rachel's delirium at the end produces a vision of her own drowning, possibly inspired by Woolf's thoughts about the drowned victims of the *Titanic* disaster and oddly anticipating her own death years later. But in this vision, drowning does not mean death but a kind of protective withdrawal: 'while all her tormentors thought that she was dead, she was not dead, but curled up at the bottom of the sea' (*vo*, 398). Indirectly, this passage echoes the ending of Kate Chopin's *The Awakening* (1899), where the heroine Edna Pontellier finds the allure of the sea and drowning a relief from a challenging, troubling life. The water 'of the Gulf', we read, 'stretched out before her, gleaming with the million lights of the sun. The voice of the sea is seductive, never ceasing, whispering, clamouring, murmuring, inviting the soul to wander in the abyss of solitude.' Standing naked on the beach, she slowly walks into the water, the 'touch of the sea . . . enfolding the body in its soft, close embrace'. The final paragraph begins, 'she looked into the distance, and the old terror flamed up for an instant, then sank again.'[7]

An earlier account than *The Voyage Out* involving water and death is found in Woolf's story of 'The Serpentine', which appears in her journal for 1903, about the discovery that September of the body of a woman who had committed suicide in the lake that curls across Hyde Park. Written when she was 21, it anticipates her own actions almost three decades later. Woolf elaborates on the reported discovery, imagining a life for the woman and expanding upon the details of the incident by adding a note found pinned to the inside of the woman's dress: 'No father, no mother, no work'.[8] In *A Room of One's Own*, Woolf envisions Judith, a sister of Shakespeare, with equal talent to her famous brother but lost, without the opportunities for a career in the theatre because she is a woman.

Water remained a metaphor and a fear throughout Woolf's life. Fearful of being unable to write again once she completed a work,

Virginia Woolf reading in the garden at Garsington in June 1926, photograph by Lady Ottoline Morrell.

she would immediately begin to plan another – for fear of drowning: 'The only way I keep afloat is by working . . . directly I stop working I feel that I am sinking down, down. And as usual, I feel that if I sink further I shall reach the truth' (*D*, III, 235). Sinking under water, drowning, was a great source of dread but, in an unexpected way, also Woolf's salvation. Sitting with her writing board, she explains,

> I let myself down, like a diver, very cautiously into the last
> sentence I wrote yesterday. Then perhaps after 20 minutes
> or it may be more, I shall see a light in the depths of the sea,

and stealthily approach – for one's sentences are only an
approximation, a net one flings over some sea pearl which
may vanish. (*LETT*, IV, 223)

In 'A Sketch of the Past', composed in the summer of 1939 when
thinking of her half-sister Stella, Woolf remarks that

The past only comes back when the present runs so smoothly
that it is like the sliding surface of a deep river. Then one
sees through the surface to the depths. . . . [the] present
when backed by the past is a thousand times deeper than
the present when it presses so close that you can feel nothing
else, when the film on the camera reaches only the eyes.[9]

To get to the depths is Woolf's goal.

From the outset, Woolf's literary aims rejected the Edwardian
complacency inherited from the Victorians – a desire rendered
by Lily Briscoe in *To the Lighthouse*, in terms of what the character
rejects and pursues: 'Beautiful pictures. Beautiful phrases. But what
she wished to get hold of was that very jar on the nerves, the thing
itself before it has been made anything' (*TL*, 158). For Woolf, this is
the *raison d'être* of the writer, especially the female writer. But the
'jar on the nerves' may allude to her own mental illness, which more
or less followed the death of her mother from rheumatic fever when
she was thirteen. At the same time it gave impetus to her writing
and the creation of a series of vital, independent women, from
Katharine Hilbery of *Night and Day* to Mrs Dalloway, Mrs Ramsay
in *To the Lighthouse*, Eleanor Pargiter (*The Years*), Miss La Trobe
(*Between the Acts*) and even Orlando.

However, the question remains: was Woolf's mental illness
a spur or an obstacle to her writing? The answer – or answers
– are complicated. Her illness was partly generated by the deaths,
in a short period of time, of her mother, her half-sister (Stella),

her father and her brother, all by the time she was only 24 years old. Her half-brother Gerald sexually molested her, while another half-sister from her father's first marriage (Laura) was institutionalized in 1891. Art became a means to confront but not always transcend these setbacks. As she would later write, 'I meant to write about death, only life came breaking in as usual' (*D*, III, 167).

Alongside examining this theme of writing as therapy, the following chapters will look at Woolf's use and need of place – the ever-recurring value of 'A Room of One's Own', the title of her Cambridge lectures of 1928. Ever since she was a child, Woolf understood the link between creativity and location. Her early summer trips to Talland House in St Ives, recalled fictionally in *To the Lighthouse*, are only one of numerous memories of the importance of finding a space to think, to play and later to write in. But the focus on place as establishing the context for writing is not so much a physical as a psychological space: for a writer, place 'is a territory within his own brain', more real than anything of brick or mortar, as she explains in her essay 'Literary Geography'.[10] The opening of her very first novel foregrounds this new world of space and place; *The Voyage Out* begins with a description of London and the streets leading from the Strand down to the Embankment and includes the telling line suggestive of isolation, because the streets 'are very narrow, it is better not to walk down them [the passage-ways] arm-in-arm' (*VO*, 3). But, as the residential addresses that link themselves with Woolf attest, where she was defined who she might become. Repeatedly, she needed to become a part of these places to reaffirm her identity, which simultaneously remained rooted and yet evolved. The May visit to the *Titanic* inquiry coincided, however, with a critical, life-changing event: on 29 May 1912, she accepted Leonard's marriage proposal. They wed on 10 August; she was 30, he was 31.

Even in the age of the telephone, Woolf wrote prolifically – letters, diaries, journals, essays, memoirs. The best author of her biography is herself, in the six volumes of her letters, 38 years of diaries (published in five volumes with the sixth an early journal) and six volumes of her essays. The novels themselves also contain autobiographical elements. Yet a narrative of her journey from the daughter of one of the nineteenth century's most important if conventional men of letters – Sir Leslie Stephen – to one of the most unconventional but internationally recognized writers is constantly fascinating and needs to be retold. But while we have remarkable documentation of her life – and knowledge of details such as a list of the quartets she once heard at a London chamber music concert – it is the shape and disruptions of her life that we need to review to understand Woolf's arc as an artist. As she herself noted, what makes a biography succeed is 'the record of the things that change rather than of the things that happen'.[11]

In her early life, Virginia Stephen's houseguests ranged from James Russell Lowell (her godfather) to Thomas Hardy, John Addington Symonds and Henry James; she later met and befriended T. S. Eliot, W. B. Yeats, Katherine Mansfield, Rebecca West and Sigmund Freud. This is a woman who announces, determinedly, in her diary in November 1928, 'I will read Proust', and does (*D*, III, 209). But one cannot escape the psychological dimension of her artistic and personal needs. To a friend she writes that her brain is 'washed with the most violent waves of emotion. What about? I don't know. It begins on waking; and I never know which – shall I be happy? Shall I be miserable?' (*LETT*, III, 245). But writing was more than a panacea: 'Once the mind gets hot it can't stop; I walk making up phrases; sit, contriving scenes; am in short in the thick of the greatest rapture known to me' (*D*, III, 161).

1

22 Hyde Park Gate, 1882–1904

What cuts the deepest channels in our lives are the different houses
in which we live – deeper even than 'marriage and death and division',
so that the chapters of one's autobiography should be determined by
the different periods in which one has lived in different houses.

Leonard Woolf, *Beginning Again* (1964)

Adeline Virginia Stephen was born on 25 January 1882, the same
year as James Joyce, Wyndham Lewis and A. A. Milne – as well
as Franklin D. Roosevelt, Melanie Klein, Samuel Goldwyn and
Igor Stravinsky. Pablo Picasso was born the year before and John
Maynard Keynes the year after. The year also marked the deaths
of Charles Darwin, Anthony Trollope and Dante Gabriel Rossetti,
signalling the end of an era. That same year Oscar Wilde arrived
in America for his first reading tour, an assassination attempt
on Queen Victoria – the last of seven attempts over the course of
her reign – failed, the Phoenix Park murders occurred in Dublin,
Wagner's *Parsifal* debuted at the Bayreuth *Festspielhaus* in Bavaria
and Tchaikovsky's *1812 Overture* had its first performance in Moscow.

Virginia Stephen was born at the home of her parents, Sir Leslie
Stephen and Julia Duckworth Stephen, on a cul-de-sac off Kensington
Road between Palace Gate and Queen's Gate. No. 22 Hyde Park Gate
was located towards the bottom end of the dead-end street that
would become home to Winston Churchill at No. 28 and Sir Jacob
Epstein at No. 18. Kensington was something of the family village,

since Leslie Stephen was born at 42 Hyde Park Gate in 1832 and, in late 1875, shortly after the death of his first wife 'Minny' Thackeray (with whom he had a daughter, Laura Stephen, who was mentally challenged), Stephen moved into 11 Hyde Park Gate South, (later 20 Hyde Park Gate). Julia Prinsep Duckworth, widowed after her husband Herbert Duckworth had died in 1870, lived at 13 Hyde Park Gate. Julia had been a widow eight years, Leslie three, when the two married in 1878; Leslie was fifteen years older than his new wife. In March 1878 they settled at 13 Hyde Park Gate which, renumbered, became 22 Hyde Park Gate in 1884.

The Stephens' home was narrow, dark and high. The blending of the Duckworth and Stephen families, including Laura Stephen and Julia's three children – George, Stella and Gerald – meant a full household even before they had four more children of their own, only two of whom were intended: Vanessa in 1879, Thoby in 1880 and then, as 'afterthoughts', Virginia in 1882 and Adrian in 1883. Together, there were eight children between them, like the Ramsays in *To the Lighthouse*.

At the top, Hyde Park Gate opened out to busy Kensington Road, which became High Street Kensington to the west, and faced Kensington Gardens; No. 22 had two added storeys at the top with a Dutch gable roof and a dining-room extension at the back. The numerous small, oddly shaped rooms, the plans having been sketched by Virginia's mother to save architect's fees, meant six or seven servants crammed into a home with only one bathroom and three water closets. The basement was given to the cook, Sophie Farrell (who would go to 46 Gordon Square and then to 29 Fitzroy Square with Woolf after Leslie Stephen died), and other servants. The ground floor was for the family, who entertained in a large double room with a dining room just off it. Leslie and Julia's double bedroom, with a nursery next door, was on the first floor. Above were three bedrooms for George, Stella and Gerald. On the third floor was a day and night nursery for the Stephen children as

Vanessa Stephen   Stella Duckworth   Virginia Stephen

The three Stephen sisters: Vanessa, Stella Duckworth (half-sister) and Virginia, *c.* 1896.

they got older and at the top of the house, in a large airy study, was their father's library and workspace. At the house's apex, under the roof, the servants lived in shabby attic bedrooms. Today, the home has been divided into six flats and has three blue plaques to the left of the main entrance. These read in descending order: Sir Leslie Stephen, Vanessa Bell and Virginia Woolf.

The decor was dark with heavy Victorian drapes on the windows. There was no electricity and most rooms could only be seen by daylight or candle- or lamplight. Chippendale furniture, portraits of family members, a chest in the hallway with a silver salver 'deep in visiting cards' and daily gatherings around the tea table in the late afternoon were part of the daily rituals of the household.[1] Julia Stephen covered the furniture in red velvet and painted the wood-work black with thin gold lines, later changed to raspberry – a feature of Jacob's lodgings in *Jacob's Room*. There were busts framed by crimson velvet and dark oil portraits. A thick curtain of Virginia creeper hung over the back drawing-room window, obscuring the outside view. The street in front was unusually quiet since it was a cul-de-sac, but the eight children, two parents and collection of servants likely made up for the lack of noise and activity outside. Despite the interior gloom, it could sometimes be a warm household, with the father affectionately referring to Vanessa and Virginia as 'Nessa' and 'Ginia'.

One of the bright spots of the home was music: Julia Stephen played the piano and in 1902 they owned a pianola, which played regularly after dinner to the delight of the children (*LETT*, I, 57). A family acquaintance who often visited was Sir Hubert Parry, director of the Royal College of Music, and no less than the French musician Arnold Dolmetsch (a friend of Ezra Pound's) taught Virginia's half-sister Stella Duckworth the violin. Virginia and Vanessa were taught the piano and had singing lessons, although Virginia early on pronounced herself unmusical. When older, she became aware of differences in the education of men versus women

No. 22 Hyde Park Gate.

The Stephen siblings (from left, Adrian, Thoby, Vanessa and Virginia) with dog, shown on holiday at Look-out Point, St Ives, *c.* 1892.

regarding music, and criticized the inequality in her 1920 essay 'The Intellectual Status of Women'. In a later letter, she noted that in her youth there was not a single woman in an orchestra and that there seemed to be prejudice against women and limited opportunities for professional musical education. Her friendship with the composer Ethel Smyth likely shaped her views. In 1940 Virginia Woolf wrote in a letter: 'I always think of my books as music before I write them', although she prefaced the remark by saying, 'I'm not regularly musical' (*LETT*, VI, 426). Her attendance at operas and concerts increased after the turn of the century, and by 1907 she was attending performances three or four times a week.[2]

Hyde Park Gate was the shaping force of an extinct life, and one that Woolf would shed in 1904 following the death of her father. But for her first 22 years, formal behaviour – dressing every night at 7.30 pm for dinner at 8 pm – especially with guests, reigned. Childhood Kensington, described in 'A Sketch of the Past', was a consummate 'literate, letter-writing, visiting, articulate late 19th-century world'.[3] The house itself was divided into separate spheres, broadly defined as male and female. The children were residents of the day and night nurseries on the upper floors, although despite the divisions there was a general lack of privacy, which was especially noticeable during adolescence. Their father's study was above and they would often hear him speaking out loud as he wrote or even the sound of him dropping books would reverberate through the floor. His library was huge and included the great works of English and European literature; his three-volume series *Hours in a Library* (1892) and even his epistolary memoir, *Mausoleum Book*, document his readings and holdings. This was not a closed-off space, however; he gladly opened his sanctuary to his inquisitive daughter Ginia.

Leslie and Julia Stephen reading, with daughter Virginia Stephen, aged 11, watching, 1893. Photograph taken at their Hyde Park Gate home by Vanessa Stephen.

Recalling her youth, Woolf wrote that her childhood had been divided into only two large spaces, one spent 'indoors in the drawing room and nursery, and the other in Kensington Gardens'. Life was not 'crowded with events' but 'ordered with great simplicity and regularity'.[4] Part of the youthful excitement at Hyde Park Gate had to do with the arrival of the collaborative weekly the *Hyde Park Gate News*, an effort by Virginia, Thoby and Vanessa. Every Monday morning, it landed on their mother's breakfast plate. The paper appeared weekly from 9 February 1891 until April 1895, ceasing publication shortly after Julia Stephen died. It was originally a joint venture between the Stephen siblings but it gradually became almost entirely Virginia's responsibility. Articles and stories ranged from mock journalism to 'An Easy Alphabet for Infants'. Woolf's delight in her mother's pleasure with her stories was unbounded.

In 'A Sketch of the Past', she admits that her mother, both while she was alive and after, 'obsessed' her: 'I could hear her voice, see her, imagine what she would do or say as I went about my day's doing.' She was an 'invisible presence' who almost never left her, until the age of 44 when she wrote *To the Lighthouse*. She had been 'in the very centre of that great Cathedral space which was childhood' until Woolf was able to express deeply held emotions in her novel. And importantly, Woolf links her mother to place: 'she was the whole thing; Talland House was full of her; Hyde Park Gate was full of her.'[5] She was the centre of family life, which was constantly busy and crowded with people.

After being widowed from his first marriage, Leslie Stephen, already recognized as a notable essayist and man of letters as well as a pioneering Alpinist, first asked Julia Duckworth to marry him in a letter. She quickly refused him, but one night, when he was dining with her in order to seek advice regarding his first daughter Laura, she escorted him to the door when he was leaving and said she would try to be a good wife. And for the next seventeen years, she was.[6]

But that all changed on 5 May 1895 when, aged 49, Julia Stephen died. Suddenly, there was quiet, calm and sadness, a grief that became the new tone at Hyde Park Gate. Indeed, the notepaper used to reply to sympathy notes had such a thick black border that only a small space remained for writing. There were no more parties. The tragedy of her death, Woolf writes in 'A Sketch of the Past', was not that it made one unhappy but that it made her mother 'unreal; and us solemn, and self-conscious. We were made to act parts that we did not feel.'[7] The conventions of enacting sorrow and mournful behaviour overrode their actual feelings.

Other deaths also disrupted Woolf's youth, notably the deaths of her half-sister Stella Duckworth in 1897, her father in 1904 and then her brother Thoby in 1906. Stella, who had been looking after the Stephen household when her mother was away, quickly assumed many of the family duties after her mother died, trying to comfort her father while managing and running the household. As a child, Stella was devoted to her mother, who ironically treated her severely, partly because they were so alike. Woolf referred to the two as the 'sun and moon to each other: my mother the positive and definite; Stella the reflecting and satellite'. Stella was outside the orbit of her mother's love, which was instead concentrated on Stella's brother, George.[8] But, uncomplaining and unselfish, Stella quickly took over the maternal role.

Woolf was less sympathetic to her two stepbrothers, George and Gerald, than she was to Stella, describing them as 'opaque and conventional'.[9] Stella had rheumatic fever as a child which may have slightly impeded her ability in later life to learn, but it did not affect her commitment to the Stephen family, including visits to Laura Stephen, possibly psychotic and by then institutionalized, although in the 1880s she lived apart from the rest of the family at 22 Hyde Park Gate. In 1906 the four Stephen children mortgaged 22 Hyde Park Gate, raising £489 for Laura's living expenses. Stella also took responsibility for Woolf during her breakdown following her mother's death.

Stella had various suitors, although she initially rejected the solicitor Jack Hills, for many years the Stephens' family lawyer, which led to a serious breach between the two families; Woolf

Virginia (left) and Vanessa Stephen playing cricket, St Ives, 1894.

compared premarital relations to diplomatic negotiations of the highest order.[10] Jack Hills, protégé of Julia Prinsep Stephen, had proposed to Stella Duckworth in the 1890s but was not at first accepted. He proposed again after Julia Stephen died and Stella finally accepted. Vanessa and Virginia were bridesmaids at Stella and Jack's wedding on 10 April 1897. But in July, returning early from their honeymoon in Italy, Stella died at 27 Hyde Park Gate from peritonitis complicated by pregnancy. Prue Ramsay evokes Stella in *To the Lighthouse*, her early and unexpected death an echo of Stella's sudden demise. Again, Woolf found death surrounding her.

Virginia and Vanessa comforted Jack following Stella's death, while he blamed Leslie Stephen for delaying their engagement through jealousy. During this time Vanessa became intimate with him and they appeared to have fallen in love. However, in England at that time it was illegal for a man to marry his deceased wife's sister, and the affair soon dwindled. In 'A Sketch of the Past' Woolf writes that Stella's engagement to Jack gave Woolf her 'first vision of love between man and woman . . . it was to me like a ruby . . . glowing red, clear, intense'. Jack, a country gentleman who wrote several books on fishing, became an MP after his years as a lawyer from 1906 to 1922, and he was also re-elected in 1925. After Stella's death, Jack continued to visit Woolf, becoming the first man to speak openly to her about sex after she moved to 29 Fitzroy Square (discussed in Chapter Three), with its green carpet and 'red Chinese curtains', in 1907.[11]

Before her father's illness, Woolf and her sister were educated at home by their mother Julia, who tutored both girls, while their father unsuccessfully lectured them in maths. When Vanessa went to art school, Woolf remained at home alone, studying Greek, writing in her diary or reading classics from her father's extensive library. When Vanessa was home, they would spend time together, but after Stella's death, it rested on Vanessa to become the female head of the house. Suddenly, Vanessa had to organize the servants every morning and keep household accounts, as well as being responsible for the general upkeep of the home. She reluctantly accepted these duties, internally opposing, through silence and an air of angry unhappiness, her father's harshness.[12] But in expressing her constant sympathy to Jack Hills over his loss, she became enamoured with him, although the law and the Duckworth brothers brought it to an end.

Nervous and insecure, Woolf had to adjust to her older sister making independent decisions. A diary often became her refuge. Started when she was fourteen, in 1897, the diaries contain entries until four days before her suicide at age 59 in 1941. There are 38 handwritten volumes, forming her longest work, the passages a doorway to her fiction. In her earliest years, she crated and bound the books herself, and for her 1903 diary not only formed chapters but made a table of contents. The first of the five collected diary volumes was published in 1977, with the following four volumes published in instalments until 1984. In 1990 the sixth and final volume – *A Passionate Apprentice: The Early Journals, 1897–1909* – appeared.[13] The volumes reflect three stages of growth: experimental early diaries from 1897 to 1918, a set of 'modernist diaries' from 1919 to 1929 and, finally, entries from the years 1930 to 1941, a period of almost constant writing and worry. Throughout this period, Woolf educated herself in the diaries of others, beginning with Sir Walter Scott and Fanny Burney before starting her own first effort. In the period before her half-sister Stella married she read Samuel Pepys, referring to him as 'the only calm thing in the house',[14] and at the age of 21 she read James Boswell's *Journal of a Tour to the Hebrides* (1785), returning to these figures repeatedly throughout her life. She also wrote reviews of others' diaries and of journals and essays that dealt with the diary as a literary form.[15] Importantly, nearly a third of the diaries Woolf read were by women, and these became a vital source of her understanding of women's lives. Mary Coleridge was especially important, as was Mary Seton Berry, a powerful voice for women's rights. The shy and nervous young writer discovered that other would-be writers had similar doubts about their skill and place in the world, but could express themselves privately in their diaries.

The impact of Stella's death was to solidify the relationships between the four Stephen children: Thoby (two years older and a natural artist), Adrian, Vanessa and Virginia. The siblings became dearer to each other, and their close bond became a barrier, a protection against the distressing tragedies and death that would befall the family. Their relationship formed the nexus and forged the model of Woolf's friendships in later life; she learned to partly emulate Thoby's 'great power for admiring his friends'.[16] The subsequent death of Leslie Stephen, at his home on 22 February 1904, was an equally shattering experience that similarly bonded the children. Woolf's father, whom she called 'difficult, exacting, [and] dependent' on his wife, had entered an extended period of grief after Julia's death: whenever he spoke, which was not often, he ended his sentences with a groan.[17] Without deviation, he assumed the pose of a lonely, deserted, unhappy man who was hurt and possessive and even jealous of young men like Jack Hills. He was selfish and delayed Stella's marriage and exploded when Stella told him that she and Hills would not live at 22 Hyde Park Gate, although they did move into No. 27. Leslie Stephen, who had been entirely emotionally dependent on his wife, let the burden of his dependency fall to his children. He would die of stomach cancer aged 72.[18] In 'A Sketch of the Past', at the end of a paragraph summarizing her mother's life and death, Woolf recounts how her father 'staggered from the bedroom as we came [in the hall]. I stretched out my arms to stop him, but he brushed past me . . . distraught.' She would never forget that moment. Only being taken to Paddington a day or so later to meet her brother Thoby, returning for the funeral from Clifton College, a public school in Bristol (which Roger Fry also attended), and recalling the blaze of sunlight through the glass dome of the station in stark contrast to the dark and curtained rooms of Hyde Park Gate, brought any relief to her own sorrow.[19]

In the same passage in her memoir, Woolf refers to a similar moment with her sister Vanessa in nearby Kensington Gardens when she (Woolf) read a poem on the grass and for the first time understood poetry: 'I had a feeling of transparency in words when they cease to be words and become so intensified that one seems to experience them.' But a dark cloud descended over their formerly active family life with the death of their mother. Instead of 'the arch of glass burning at the end of Paddington Station', there was a 'cooped up, sad, solemn, real' life 'under a haze of heavy emotion'.[20] A shrouded life descended, which would last some nine years.

Yet from her father Woolf inherited industriousness, determination, a love of books and a commitment to writing. Like him, she began as a journalist, or more precisely a reviewer and essayist, with her earliest work appearing in the weekly *Guardian* in 1904. But Leslie was also a hard blend of sensitivity and harshness, the two often in conflict. His sense of failure and self-pity upset the young Woolf, who would later share his lack of self-confidence. Yet his realization that she had a genuine appreciation of literature and a curiosity about writing warmed him to her. They would often go on long walks around the Serpentine and she inherited from him her later love of walking through London, frequently for two hours a day. A commemorative article by Woolf in *The Times* celebrating Leslie's centenary in 1932 presented a sympathetic and generous portrait of her father, emphasizing his intellectual energy and her literary debt to him for allowing her free rein of his library from the age of fifteen.

Leslie's death caused Woolf her most extreme mental breakdown to date. Woolf was virtually her father's only close companion during the last two years of his life. She spent part of each day sitting with him, while nurses dealt with his medical needs, his deafness no hindrance to their mutual understanding. Vanessa was away most days studying at art college or visiting friends; Thoby and Adrian were away at the University of Cambridge, while George and Gerald Duckworth were busy with their careers. Four days after Leslie died, Woolf took out a lifetime membership to the London Library – of which he had been president from 1892 until his death – perhaps as an acknowledgement of his lasting literary influence on her. When taken to the library as a young girl, Woolf remarked to her father that all the pictures she saw were of men. She remembered those images when she began to address the status of women in the public realm, in works such as *A Room of One's Own*. Earlier in November 1903, as he was weakening, Stephen dictated the final pages of his *Mausoleum Book* to Woolf, the autobiography begun shortly after Julia Stephen died in 1895.

Leslie Stephen had dominated the lives of the girls after their mother's death until his own death. As Woolf famously wrote in her diary in 1928 concerning her father's death, 'his life would have entirely ended mine. What would have happened? No writing, no books; – inconceivable' (*D*, III, 208). Nevertheless, Woolf could tell a friend in 1924 that 'we Stephens are difficult, especially as the race tapers out, towards its finish – such cold fingers, so fastidious, so critical, such taste' (*LETT*, III, 92–3). In 'A Sketch of the Past' she also noted that she and her sister and brother 'lived under the sway of a society that was about fifty years too old for us. It was this curious fact that made our struggle so bitter and so violent.' She and her sister 'were living say in 1910; they [her two stepbrothers] were living in 1860.'[21]

Vanessa's view of Hyde Park Gate was not as dark or as intense as her sister's, who tended to use an anatomical model for her reminiscence, often focusing on the first-floor bedroom – 'the sexual centre; the birth centre, the death centre of the house'. It was not a large room 'but its walls must be soaked, if walls take pictures'.[22] When she visited the home on 30 January 1905 following a luncheon with Margaret Duckworth, she noted in her journal that her old room was 'so strange with the ink splashes & shelves as of old. I could write the history of every mark & scratch in that room where I lived so long.'[23] 'The place seemed tangled and matted with emotion', she wrote in 'Old Bloomsbury', suggesting how she would treat space and a home in *To the Lighthouse*.[24] Vanessa's memoirs of the past parallel her sister's. In 'Life at Hyde Park Gate after 1897', written before 1941, and 'Notes on Bloomsbury' from 1951, Vanessa repeats Woolf's views, but where Woolf offers an almost visceral sense of claustrophobia, Vanessa offers a more chiaroscuro view. She observes, with an artist's eye, the thick Virginia creeper that came down over the drawing room windows, blocking light. The house itself seemed to be in mourning with its black paint and dull blue walls absorbing all light.[25]

For Woolf, her father's death was a liberating event for her writing life, highlighted by her departure from the Victorian confines of Hyde Park Gate to the open and less restricted world of 46 Gordon Square – in less respectable Bloomsbury. But before she could adjust to this major change, Woolf went through a second period of mental illness, beginning in May 1904; she was 22 years old. Initially under the care of Dr George Savage, author of *Insanity and Allied Neuroses* (1884), she went to the home of Violet Dickinson (a friend of Stella Duckworth) in Burnham Wood for nearly three months. During this period she made her first attempt at suicide by trying to throw herself from a window. Ten years earlier, Thoby had attempted to throw himself out of a window while at Clifton.

Woolf at this time was establishing new and vital friendships to replace the strained family unit at 22 Hyde Park Gate. One of the most important of these relationships was with Violet Dickinson, who was seventeen years Woolf's senior and supposedly 1.88 metres (6 feet 2 inches) tall, and who likely met Woolf in 1897. She was known for her generosity, good works (which included improving the conditions of mentally ill women) and being badly dressed. Her Quaker background prompted her interest in helping others, especially women who suffered social injustices. In 1902 she began to correspond with Woolf, and her common sense, optimism and practicality balanced the gloom that often inhabited Hyde Park Gate. She and Woolf would holiday together in Venice, Florence and Paris. 'Friendship's Gallery' (1907), a mock biography of Dickinson by Woolf, is partly about their attachment. During Leslie Stephen's decline, Woolf wrote daily bulletins on his health to Dickinson. Woolf became closer to Dickinson after her father's death and in turn Dickinson became a strong believer in Woolf's literary talent. She soon introduced her to Margaret Lyttelton, editor of the women's supplement to *The Guardian*, who as a result commissioned Woolf to write an article on Charlotte Brontë. Her first publication in the paper, however, was a review of a volume of social history, followed by a review of W. D. Howells's *The Son of Royal Langbrith* on the 14 December 1904. Her piece on Brontë, 'Haworth, November 1904', appeared in print on 21 December 1904.

Dickinson became one of Woolf's closest friends – a friendship that followed Dickinson's cherished relationship with Kate Greenaway, the children's author, who died in 1901. Woolf read the biography of Greenaway by M. H. Spielman of 1905 and felt jealous; her letters to Dickinson suddenly became more emotional. The biography also emphasized how Greenaway had been in constant fear of losing her friends, a feeling which transferred to Woolf. In 1906 Dickinson travelled with Woolf and Vanessa to Greece where they met Adrian and Thoby Stephen. Dickinson continued to support Woolf, who valued her constant encouragement, and Woolf celebrated her 25th birthday with Dickinson at Burnham Wood. At about this time, Woolf had prepared Dickinson's mock biography, which was presented to her in August, typed in violet ink – the colour resembles J. Herbin's Violette Pensée or possibly Waterman's Violet – and bound in violet leather. The habit of writing in violet or purple ink remained with Woolf throughout her life as a tribute to Dickinson and her influence on her work, plus a friendship of some 42 years, although this would diminish in intensity over the years.[26]

Much later, after Woolf finished her first novel *The Voyage Out* in 1913, she wrote an exuberant letter to Dickinson, whom she saw little of once she married Leonard in 1912. Indeed, their attachment began to subside in about 1908. Records also show that just before Woolf's death, she had all the letters Dickinson sent her over the years destroyed, leaving unanswered the question of an early, intimate relationship with Dickinson, who, importantly, kept all those written by Woolf to her. In Dickinson, however, as with Vita Sackville-West and Ethel Smyth later on, Woolf sought a certain maternal love that had been absent in her life since the death of her mother when she was thirteen. All three women, plus her sister Vanessa, became cherished confidantes and her friendships with these women would influence her works to come.

Another early and important female friend was Madge Symonds (later Vaughan), the vivacious daughter of John Addington Symonds. Thirteen years older than Woolf, Symonds was the first to learn of Woolf's literary ambitions, and she would be the inspiration for Sally Seton in *Mrs Dalloway*. Woolf called her a woman 'full of theories and emotions, and innumerable questions' and apparently had a crush on her (*LETT*, I, xviii, 88). Janet Case, another companion, with whom Woolf studied Greek from 1902 to 1903 (Woolf began learning Greek with Clara Pater, sister of Walter Pater), also became a lifelong friend. Woolf was initially introduced to Greek thought through Thoby, and her admiration for the language as an entry to classical culture remained throughout her life.[27] In 1907 Woolf wrote, 'I write in the morning and read Pindar', while Adrian 'spells out Wagner on the piano' (*LETT*, I, 308). In *The Voyage Out*, Mrs Dalloway remarks, in the midst of a debate concerning art versus politics, that she could never forget a production of *Antigone* seen at Cambridge. '"Don't you think it's quite the most modern thing you ever saw?"' she asks Ridley

Ambrose, travelling so that he may work on his edition of Pindar in the novel (he is a former Cambridge don who lives in London where he edits the classics). When Mr Pepper replies in six lines of Greek quoted from the second chorus of *Antigone*, Mrs Dalloway compresses her lips and says "'I'd give ten years of my life to know Greek'" (*VO*, 44). Ridley replies, "'I could teach you the alphabet in half an hour; you could read Homer in a month'" (*VO*, 45). Fancifully, Mrs Dalloway imagines herself in her drawing room in London with 'a Plato open on her knees – Plato in the original Greek' (*VO*, 45), and when she falls asleep in her cabin she dreams of being visited by 'great Greek letters stalking round the room' (*VO*, 53). Awaking, she transposes the letters to real people sleeping in adjacent cabins. In *The Years*, Edward Pargiter will read *Antigone* at Oxford (for a moment imagining his cousin Kitty as both Antigone and his cousin), while North Pargiter will re-encounter his uncle Edward, who edits Sophocles late in the novel (*Y*, 49, 50, 385).

Jacob's Room repeatedly celebrates the Greeks: 'when all's said and done, when one's rinsed one's mouth with every literature in the world . . . it's the flavour of Greek that remains', claims Durrant as he and Jacob walk down Haverstock Hill (*JR*, 101). Fittingly, Jacob visits Greece, spending time in both the countryside and Athens, and continues to allude to Greece throughout the latter part of the novel, with as much ambiguity as certainty: 'Jacob . . . drew a plan of the Parthenon in the dust in Hyde Park, a network of strokes at least, which may have been the Parthenon, or again a mathematical diagram' (*JR*, 236). Sometimes Greece evokes danger in the novel, as when Woolf writes that 'darkness drops like a knife over Greece' (*JR*, 245). Even in Woolf's playful writing, as in her biography of Elizabeth Barrett Browning's spaniel Flush, she cannot escape Greek. Ensconced in Miss Barrett's back parlour, Flush safely rests with his head 'pillowed on a Greek lexicon'. Earlier, as Flush ponders the frustration of his inability to communicate in words as he witnesses Elizabeth Barrett's sadness, he wonders if she is 'no longer an invalid in Wimpole Street, but a Greek nymph in some dim grove in Arcady'.[28]

'On Not Knowing Greek', Woolf's lengthy essay of 1925 published in the first series of *The Common Reader*, reflects her careful reading of Sophocles, Euripides, Aristophanes and Aeschylus and alludes to her own translation and text of Aeschylus' *Agamemnon* (*D*, II, 215). In preparation for the essay, she read Homer, Plato and biographies of various classicists. But despite her study, she remained uncertain of her abilities. In the essay she explains that since we can never recreate the language or style of Greek completely, it is impossible to know it. We will never learn how it was originally spoken or acted. Reading Greek drama means reading it as poetry since the exact meaning of the words escapes us; we will never know 'how the words sounded' or 'how the actors acted'.[29] How strange, then, is our desire to know Greek. But we do wish to understand the culture and the impersonal nature of the language. 'On Not Knowing Greek' is as much a commentary on English society and its customs as it is of the Greek language. But comparisons between the two cultures exist. The way each stage movement signifies in Greek drama finds a parallel in the critical actions of characters in Jane Austen, such as in *Emma* when a young cousin (Henry) steps forward to 'rescue' Louisa and says clearly and simply, 'I will dance with you.'[30] This is an act of both freedom and submission, all the more important because, as in Greek drama, characters are bound and restricted to limited actions. Woolf also compares Greek drama to Proust in the essay, arguing that in six pages of Proust 'we can find more complicated and varied emotions than in the whole of the *Electra.*' In Proust we find something greater: 'heroism itself' and fidelity. What draws us back to the Greeks is that 'the stable, the permanent, the original human being is to be found there'. Antigone, Ajax and Electra are originals and we understand them more 'easily and more directly' than the characters in *The Canterbury Tales*. For Woolf, the Greek figures are originals, while Chaucer's characters are only varieties. Even without forerunners or literary schools to trace its evolution, Greek is 'the literature of masterpieces'.[31]

Supplementing Woolf's interest in Greek was her support of the women's suffrage movement, another of Janet Case's causes. Case offered a political corrective to Woolf's growing aestheticism and, more importantly, a deep, sustaining friendship; in 1911 Case spent a weekend with Woolf at Little Talland House in Sussex, where Woolf revealed to her the incestuous actions of her half-brother George (*LETT*, I, 472). Woolf remained in contact with Case until her death in 1937, publishing an unsigned obituary of her in *The Times*. In her diary Woolf confided 'how great a visionary part she has played in my life' (*D*, V, 103). As Woolf would also remark in *The Voyage Out*, 'just consider: it's the beginning of the twentieth century, and until a few years ago no woman had ever come out by herself and said things at all' (*VO*, 245).

Among Woolf's closest confidantes was her sister Vanessa. Three years older and artistic, Vanessa often felt challenged by her younger sister, who wanted to be a writer early on, while Vanessa wished to be a painter. This eliminated one source of competition, as Vanessa outlined in a 1949 talk 'Notes on Virginia's Childhood', read to the Memoir Club. While Vanessa painted, Woolf would often read aloud to her. In turn, Woolf noted in 'Reminiscences' how Vanessa spoke unpleasant truths directly. An implicit rivalry emerged between the sisters, but also an emotional intimacy. Vanessa was always, as Woolf admitted, forthright. Socially, Vanessa found herself involved with a series of men, beginning with Stella's widowed husband Jack Hills. Preceding this was a trip with Violet Dickinson, Thoby and Woolf to Italy in 1904, following the death of their father, when, stopping in Paris on their return, she met Clive Bell, a Cambridge friend of Thoby's, in the studio of Rodin. They would eventually marry, although she first refused him twice. Only after Thoby's unexpected death in 1906 from typhoid fever did she agree to marry Bell, two days after her brother died. Woolf saw this

Vanessa Bell, *Virginia Woolf*, 1912, oil on board.

as a double loss – first her brother to illness and then her sister to marriage.

Vanessa, however, found Roger Fry a more understanding figure; following the birth of her second son and a miscarriage, from 1911 to 1913 the two friends had an affair. By 1914 she had fallen in love with the painter Duncan Grant, who, in fact, had had an affair with her brother Adrian. When Adrian married, Grant returned Vanessa's affection until he began a second affair with

David Garnett. Nevertheless, she lived in Suffolk with Grant and Garnett until all three moved to Charleston in Sussex in 1916. Two years later, Angelica, the child of Vanessa and Duncan Grant, would be born. Clive Bell was said to be her father and Angelica did not learn herself that Grant was her father until she was seventeen years old. Despite these unorthodox arrangements, Woolf continued to admire her sister and rely on her artistic judgement, adding that her sister's opinion of her writing was the most important to her other than Leonard's. In 1931 she told Vanessa, 'I always feel I'm writing more for you than for anybody' (*LETT*, IV, 390).

But complicating Woolf's youth (and memories) of Hyde Park Gate were the sexual actions of George Duckworth. Although the details are inconclusive, George likely accosted Woolf at age six when he was eighteen.[32] In '22 Hyde Park Gate', she records that when she was a young woman, George jumped in her bed and took her in his arms after scolding her for not behaving properly at the various dinners and gatherings he took her to, since he took responsibility for their social education.[33] As described by Woolf in her essay 'Old Bloomsbury', he would often 'fling himself on [Woolf's] bed, cuddling and kissing and otherwise embracing [her]'.[34] Much has been written about these incidents, with no single interpretation dominating other than that the episodes made a lasting impression on her, both psychologically and creatively.[35] On one hand she masked the incidents, writing of George that 'no more perfect fossil of the Victorian age could exist', but on the other she outlined the traumatic consequences of his actions.[36] Critics have suggested that he might not only be the model for Hugh Whitbread in *Mrs Dalloway* but the source of Richard Dalloway's impetuous kiss of Rachel Vinrace, which brings on nightmares, in *The Voyage Out*.

To compensate for her parents' deaths and for the ordeal of her sexual abuse by her half-brother Gerald at Talland House in Cornwall – she was earlier abused by her other half-brother George in London, both experiences leaving a lasting mark on Woolf – Woolf encouraged a long series of friendships with women. As noted, this was partly to compensate for the loss of her mother, as she turned to older women who inspired and occasionally offered the maternal love she lacked. Woolf's closest female friends were Violet Dickinson, Madge Vaughan, Janet Case, Vita Sackville-West and Ethel Smyth. Lady Ottoline Morrell, Katherine Mansfield and Dora Carrington, as well as her sister Vanessa, offered something else: examples of vibrant, independent and creative female individuals. A number of these figures would reappear in her fiction: Vanessa suggestive of Lily Briscoe in *To the Lighthouse*; Lady Ottoline Morrell as Alice Flushing, a painter who shatters propriety by smoking a cigarette at tea in *The Voyage Out*; Vita as Orlando; and Ethel Smyth as Rose Pargiter in *The Years* and as an inspiration for Miss La Trobe in *Between the Acts*. At what would be the very end of her life, Octavia Wilberforce, Woolf's final doctor, about whom Woolf would attempt a 'living portrait' in prose, became another close friend.

It is not inconceivable to develop a theory of friendship for Woolf, who found in such relationships a supplement and substitute for family. Her relationship with Leonard was based on friendship as much as love, emulating G. E. Moore's belief that sexuality was far less important than equality and mutual sympathy, which provided the true basis of love. His conclusion to *Principia Ethica* (1903) stated that 'personal affections and aesthetic enjoyments include *all* the greatest and *by far* the greatest goods that we can imagine.'[37] The aesthetic treatment of personal affections was the best way to approach these goals of friendship and commitment. Woolf and Leonard shared social, cultural and literary – although not always political – ideas that created a bond between them. The powerful nature of Woolf's friendships suggests what Deleuze calls 'the folds of friendship', constantly 'folding, unfolding and refolding', as he writes in his book on Foucault. This also describes the nature of Woolf's engagement with others.[38] Woolf actually employs the fold psychologically and metaphorically in her writing. At the end of 'On Being Ill', she uses a metonym – a crushed fold in a Victorian curtain – to communicate the agony of Lady Waterford confronting the death and burial of her husband.[39] This echoes a section of 'Reminiscences', where the young Woolf attempts to describe the death of her mother to her nephew Julian: 'Written words of a person who is dead or still alive tend most unfortunately to drape themselves in smooth folds annulling all evidence of life.'[40] For Woolf, the folds of friendship resonate with meaning and discovery.

Woolf repeatedly analysed her friendships; a diary passage from 22 January 1919 begins with 'How many friends have I got?' and proceeds to enumerate a long list of names, too many to 'put them in order'. Lytton Strachey, Desmond MacCarthy and Saxon Turner are the first three who come to mind; she ends with Ottoline Morrell, Roger Fry, Katherine Mansfield, Gilbert Murray and T. S. Eliot, whom 'I like on the strength of one visit & shall probably see more of.' And as she often did, she would write short accounts of her friends' characters: 'Lytton is said to be tolerant & less witty; Desmond, they say, needs a glass of wine; Saxon has his rheumatics & his hopeless love affair' (*D*, 1, 234–5). Woolf did not shy away from criticism of her friends, saying Strachey lacked originality and substance: his writing is 'superbly brilliant journalism' but he is 'infinitely cautious, elusive & unadventurous'. He fails to initiate the new, in contrast to her own pleasure in inventiveness: 'we Stephens, yes, & even Clive, with all his faults, had the initiative, & the vitality to conceive & carry out our wishes into effect because we wished too strongly to be chilled by ridicule or checked by difficulty' (*D*, 1, 236).

The premise of the Bloomsbury Group *was* friendship, which Woolf privileged in her fiction, even when the friendships ended. In her letters to Vita Sackville-West one finds the elements of friendship most rawly exposed. Woolf, writing to Vita on 5 February 1927, while she is in Teheran, complains that she has had no letter:

I hope this doesn't mean you have been eaten by brigands, wrecked, torn to pieces. It makes me rather dismal. It gets worse steadily – your being away. All the sleeping draughts and the irritants have worn off, and I'm settling down to wanting you, doggedly, dismally faithfully – I hope that pleases you.[41]

Friendship and love intermingle but the emotional highs and lows occur against the fabric of a sustained, lasting relationship, one that moves from trust to sharing to empathy. As Woolf wrote in *The Waves*, 'some people go to priests; others to poetry; I to my friends' (*w*, 222).

Woolf's concept of friendship may have partly originated in the Hellenic past as G. Lowes Dickinson outlined in *The Greek View of Life* (1896) and which was discussed, if not emulated, by the Cambridge Apostles, an intellectual society founded at the University in 1820 and limited to twelve members at the time – Lytton Strachey, Leonard Woolf, Saxon Turner, John Maynard Keynes and E. M. Forster were all members – and later imported into the Bloomsbury Group. Part Ten of Chapter Three of Dickinson's study is 'Friendship', stressing male love in Greek culture and legend, noting in particular Achilles and Patroclus, Socrates and Alcibiades. Most importantly, Dickinson emphasized that such love 'passed beyond persons to objective ends, linking emotion to actions in a life'.[42] Dickinson's own intense relationship with Roger Fry at Cambridge was a prelude to a long and sustained friendship.

G. E. Moore was another important figure who addressed the ethics and restated the value of friendship, in his essay 'Achilles or Patroclus?' (1894) and *Principia Ethica*. In the *Nicomachean Ethics*, Aristotle bases his definition of friendship on goodness: as Moore outlined, we choose the people we are attracted to because they are good or because we experience pleasure when around them. But strong friendships require time and familiarity. In 'Achilles or Patroclus?', Moore claims that friendship should also be based on equality, sympathy, feeling and states of consciousness – all elements Woolf would emphasize in her personal friendships and in the presentation of friendship in her fiction. Moore particularly noted that such intense friendships could be between men and men, and women and women. In Woolf's fiction, *The Waves* in particular, she extended and expanded Moore's philosophy of friendship.

Freud also had a role in Woolf's ideas of friendship. In 'Mourning and Melancholia' (1917), he argued that while mourning is a normal response to loss, melancholia is potentially a pathological response, often not to the death of someone but to the experience of losing someone or the idea of someone. Woolf experienced this with the loss of her mother, her father and then her brother Thoby. As Freud writes, mourning is the normal result not simply of the death of a loved person but also 'to the loss of . . . an abstraction taking the place of the person, such as fatherland, freedom, an ideal and so on'. Melancholia, which often accompanies mourning, can be characterized, however, by a 'profoundly painful depression, a loss of interest in the outside world, the loss of the ability to love, the inhibition of any kind of performance and a reduction in the sense of self', all qualities later displayed by Woolf.[43] Both become ways to alleviate the pain of the lost love object or the idea of a lost object, often compensated for through friendship. Of critical importance is that the loss of primary objects in childhood impacts on how we experience loss and define friendship and love in adult life. In *Civilization and Its Discontents* (1930), Freud suggests that friendship is not merely an anecdote or accessory to love or family, but of equal purpose and importance.[44]

For Woolf, friendship provided an opportunity for identification, empathy and self-understanding, overlooking social class, race or gender. From early on she valued the admiration of others: 'I am so happy that people are fond of me – you can't think . . . I do love affection!', she told Violet Dickinson (*LETT*, I, 144). Woolf enacted

Moore's theory of friendship, as well as its sense of security – an important quality of the Bloomsbury Group. As she admitted in a letter on 19 August 1930, 'take away my love for my friends . . . and I should be nothing but a membrane, a fibre, uncoloured, lifeless' (*LETT*, IV, 203). Woolf's understanding of friendship in the Hellenic past and its valuation established by Greek society shaped her own ideals. The 'politics of friendship' (the title of Derrida's study of 1994 which acknowledges Aristotle's *Ethics*, Cicero's *Laelius de amicitia* and Montaigne's 'On Friendship' as predecessors) characterizes a good deal of the Bloomsbury dynamic and Woolf's life.

Throughout their lives, Vanessa provided Woolf with both friendship and criticism and was a companion and rival. She supported Woolf in her troubling moments but also offered critiques of her work. Woolf did the same in return. Vanessa not only designed all of the book jackets for Woolf's novels after *Jacob's Room* (with the exception of *Orlando*), but was also the likely source for at least the aesthetic of Lily Briscoe in *To the Lighthouse*. Vanessa also designed the wolf's head colophon for the Hogarth Press. She drew four woodcuts for *Monday or Tuesday*, Woolf's short story collection, while her painting *A Conversation* of around 1913–16 was a possible inspiration for the story 'A Society'. She also did the illustrations for *Flush*. In turn, Woolf wrote introductions to *Recent Paintings by Vanessa Bell* (1930), and in 1934 in the catalogue for a show of Vanessa's work at the Lefevre Gallery.[45] But there remained a rivalry sometimes more pronounced than not. As young girls, the freedom-loving Vanessa contradicted the self-doubting Virginia, but when they shared a study, as they did at Hyde Park Gate and then later on occasion at Gordon Square, the competition was evident. Woolf, observing Vanessa standing at an easel to paint, would not be outdone. In response, Woolf bought a stand-up desk to write on.[46]

2

46 Gordon Square, 1904–7

Gordon Square is like nothing so much as the lions house
at the Zoo. One goes from cage to cage. All the animals are
dangerous, rather suspicious of each other, and full of fascination
and mystery.

Woolf, 23 December 1920 (*LETT*, II, 451)

With its freshly painted white walls, red carpets and new furniture,
the new home of the Stephen children – Vanessa, Virginia, Adrian
and Thoby – at 46 Gordon Square opened up their lives. Compared
to the black paint and red plush cushions framed by cabinets and
wardrobes and hoards of china and glass – the possessions of three
families that had poured into 22 Hyde Park Gate – Gordon Square
was a revelation. Tall, clean rooms with white and green chintzes
replaced the former heavy fabrics. Objects were dispersed as interior
space was reconfigured. Spaciousness and clarity were paramount.
There was a freedom of expression achieved through the agency
of things, as Woolf wrote to Madge Vaughan in 1904:

All my beloved leather backed books standing up
so handsome in their shelves . . . and a huge mass
of manuscripts and letters and proof-sheets and pens
and inks over the floor and everywhere. (*LETT*, I, 167)

In her essay 'Old Bloomsbury' she wrote,

> We were full of experiments and reforms. We were going
> to do without table napkins . . . we were going to paint; to
> write; to have coffee after dinner instead of tea at nine o'clock.
> Everything was going to be new . . . everything was on trial.[1]

Woolf was forming a writing life and space for herself. In this world freed from the shadow of Hyde Park Gate, Woolf replaced the secrecy and repression of her private life for something unrestricted and direct. They now lived close to the British Museum and the Slade School of Art, two important centres of education and art. Place now radically reordered family life but, as Woolf understood, '46 Gordon Square could never have meant what it did had not 22 Hyde Park Gate preceded it.'[2] Liberated, Bloomsbury burst forth.

The move had been planned before the death of their father. All four children had anticipated the need to free themselves from what they perceived to be the oppressive social life and atmosphere of Kensington. Virginia would later associate Kensington with a suffocating social respectability. She even disliked visiting the home of Bruce Richmond, the editor of the *Times Literary Supplement* (*TLS*), who lived across from the Natural History Museum in South Kensington, because she found the company there dreary. Only Kensington Gardens, which she often visited as a child, held her interest as an adult. Gordon Square, the new home of the Stephens, soon expanded to include artists, writers, politicians, hangers-on and lovers, not only at their Thursday evening gatherings but throughout the week and year.

The year of the move, 1904, also marked major shifts in Woolf's life. Five days after the death of Leslie Stephen she went to Manorbier on the Pembrokeshire coast for a month with her married sister Vanessa, brothers Thoby and Adrian and stepbrother George Duckworth. She also began to think of writing a book. In April she went off to Italy with Vanessa, Thoby, Adrian and Gerald Duckworth – her first trip abroad except for a childhood trip to northern France. Violet Dickinson joined them in Florence. Entertained by Clive Bell in Paris before returning home, she discovered the kind of conversation she longed for, on art, sculpture and music – what she called 'a real Bohemian party'. Also present was the artist Gerald Kelly. They met not in a drawing room but in a 'common café, while we smoked half a dozen cigarettes a piece' (*LETT*, I, 140). They also visited the studios of Rodin. The day after her return to London, Woolf experienced her second breakdown, retreating to Violet Dickinson's home to recover.

What precipitated the breakdown is not clear: was it the culmination of the trauma initiated at 22 Hyde Park Gate with the death of her mother, the death of Stella and the sexual advances of George Duckworth, or the more recent death of her father? Much has been written about Virginia's manic depression and there is no absolute answer. But the incidents were repetitive and debilitating, and this particular instance lasted for three months. Significantly, this second breakdown preceded her move to Gordon Square and her realigned life in Bloomsbury.

From 1888 to 1891, Leslie Stephen himself experienced several nervous breakdowns, although Woolf's manias and depressions would be more severe. Mood swings were unannounced and possibly observed in her father's behaviour: he was both a hypochondriac and an egotist. Woolf witnessed his own feeling of failure, and rages alternating with excitement, which she soon accepted as the price one paid to be a writer, a view supported by the family doctor, George Savage. He reinforced the neurotic genius model of Woolf by diagnosing her illness as 'neurasthenia', the identical label he used for her father.[3] Savage's remedy for Virginia was extended sleep and overfeeding to stabilize her excited brain cells (symptomatic of her depression was a refusal to eat).[4] In *Beginning Again*, Leonard Woolf outlines how her fatigue led to bouts of depression, accompanied by a constant feeling of failure.[5] To Vanessa she wrote, 'how little use I am in the world! Selfish, vain, egoistical, and incompetent' (*LETT*, I, 411).

By September 1904, Virginia was sufficiently recovered to join her family on vacation in Nottinghamshire and to resume her writing, which had stopped. In October she stayed with her aunt Caroline Emelia in Cambridge and was in close touch with her brother Adrian at Trinity College. While in Cambridge, she also began to read through and transcribe her father's letters as an aid to F. W. Maitland's biography of her father. Back in London, Vanessa and Thoby organized the move from Hyde Park Gate to Gordon Square, the Stephens having taken a lease on the property during Virginia's illness. Vanessa chose Bloomsbury in part because it was the opposite of all that Kensington stood for: rather than respectable middle-class families it was populated by students at London University or the Slade School of Art. Lodgers, not families, made up the area, which also contained 'models' and other artistic types, lending it a palpable bohemian air.

Rents in this area were also lower and although Leslie Stephen left each of his children £15,000, none of them were actually earning an income, so they all had to be prudent. In mid-September, just before the move, George Duckworth married Lady Margaret Herbert, daughter of an earl, and Gerald decided to live on his own. That same year, 1904, Leonard Woolf left Cambridge, took the Civil Service exam and sailed for Ceylon as a cadet in the Ceylon Civil Service. He prepared in part by carrying much literature with him: Desmond MacCarthy presented him with *The Oxford Miniature Shakespeare* and four volumes of Milton. On his own he purchased ninety volumes of Voltaire in an eighteenth-century edition. He left with his wire-haired terrier Charles in October.

At the same time, Woolf began her professional writing career with essays and reviews. To Violet Dickinson she wrote that 'I am longing to begin work. I know I can write . . . life interests me intensely, and writing is I know my natural means of expression' (*LETT*, I, 144). She began with book reviews, finding her voice through the reading and study of others. Non-fiction initiated her writing career and would end it: *Three Guineas* and *Roger Fry* were her last works published during her lifetime (her final fictional work, *Between the Acts*, appeared posthumously). In between were her essays, published in two volumes as *The English Common Reader* and *A Room of One's Own*.

Woolf's earliest writings are journalistic, appearing as early as 1891, when she was only nine. That year the first issue of the weekly *Hyde Park Gate News* appeared, composed and handwritten by the Stephen children. The date of her first contribution, signed Virginia Stephen, is 30 November 1891, although the paper began in April. Her very first piece is a poem, but her second, several weeks later, is a prose piece called 'A Midnight Ride', about a sick boy's younger brother, who almost gets stuck in a bog when he rides to meet his ill sibling. It ran in two successive issues. Further short stories as well as fictional letters and journals appeared in its pages. Such juvenilia, supplemented by cartoons, jokes, alphabets, riddles and correspondence, forms a backdrop to her early essay writing and reviewing.[6] One letter reads 'Miss A[deline] V[irginia] S[tephen] wants to know what the average height of men in central Australia is . . . a very big one being 5 ft 11 inches'. The next letter, from Gerald Duckworth, reads 'G.H.D. wants to know if women should vote in parliament.'[7] One of the ongoing and lengthy stories is 'The Experiences of a Paterfamilias', written with her brother Thoby and running from 10 October to 19 December 1892. The story begins with a comic account of the compulsory tricks and amusements the new father must perform for his child and ends ten chapters later with a failed shooting party.

One later text from the *Hyde Park Gate News* of 28 January 1895, author unknown, expresses the wish to be able to 'take possession of other people's minds, for a short time', something that would occur, of course, with the impact of Woolf's mature fiction.[8] Three weeks later another passage records a dream where the whole world was at the disposal of the author and 'with one stroke of

Virginia Woolf and Leslie Stephen in profile, 1902, photograph by George Charles Beresford.

my hand, the world would shiver and break and with another worlds would spring from the air.' 'I was a man alone playing with Time', reads the next sentence, prophetically predicting Woolf's later technique. Anticipating passages in her mature diary, Woolf, assuming it is Woolf, wonders if the people she creates, and even herself, are real: 'Why do I exist? . . . was everything a dream, but who were the dreamers?'[9] The four years of the *Hyde Park Gate News* (1891–5) attest to its support from the youthful family contributors, who showed no restraint in emulating the high diction and semi-technical language of more established periodicals received at their home. Remaining copies are mostly in Vanessa's hand but it was a collaborative work, although Woolf wrote most of it.[10]

Woolf had a distinguished model of literary journalism and reviewing in the house, of course: her father, who wrote for the *Saturday Review*, the *Pall Mall Gazette*, *Fraser's Magazine* and the

Fortnightly Review, among others. He had also edited the *Cornhill Magazine* from 1871 to 1882. Woolf's early efforts appear to emulate her father's work while seeking her mother's approval. Praise, always restrained in the best late Victorian manner, was celebrated when it came. With a father as an emblem of professional journalism and a mother who often offered only faint approval, one might understand Woolf's continual, persistent efforts at writerly success. However, the sudden death of her mother removed her principal reader, and Woolf did not write again for two years, only beginning again in 1897 with a personal journal.

Journalism describes Woolf's first efforts at writing, with early reviews appearing in *The Guardian* and the *TLS*. Her periodical publications appeared in *The Nation*, the *Athenaeum* and the *Criterion*, as well as more popular magazines like *Vogue* and even *Good Housekeeping*. This aspect of her writing is as valuable in understanding her career as her nine novels, not only for how essay writing became a way of polishing her prose, but because for the first ten years of her professional life her salary derived entirely from her journalism. Most of these pieces, however, were published anonymously. Nonetheless, making money and joining the literary world were her two motives for reviewing. Ironically, however, she started with a woman's supplement (in *The Guardian*) which underscored the gender bias faced by female writers. She soon branched out, however, into more mainstream publications. But even her start was an accomplishment: despite being undereducated, having uncertain health and being self-taught as a writer (through the *Hyde Park Gazette* and her early journals), she succeeded. She did, though, have an unquestioned pedigree and, through her father, connections. Woolf came to the attention of Bruce Richmond of the *TLS* because she was invited to dine with the Crums, neighbours of Violet Dickinson, to meet the esteemed editor. She was 23 years old when her writing began to appear in its pages in 1905. She contributed to the *Athenaeum* through her friendship with Katherine Mansfield, whose husband, John Middleton Murry, was its editor. Her network of women friends provided an entry point, too, and America was no different. Her u.s. agent was Ann Watkins; the editor of the *Yale Review*, where her work also appeared, was Helen McAfee. Both were important conduits for establishing Woolf's American audience. Dorothy Todd, editor of British *Vogue*, was another ally. Full of energy and ample of body, Todd was a great editor according to Rebecca West, who first met Woolf in the company of Todd and the fashion editor of *Vogue*, Madge Garland, at their Chelsea apartment.[11]

Class and social connections enhanced access for Woolf, providing associations not permitted to other women or young female journalists. Although she began by essentially writing for women, Woolf quickly found a mixed readership. Literary journalism was soon her forte, aided by editors who were friends, associates or acquaintances. By the 1920s, when she was a known and popular commodity, her journalism moved from strictly literary reviews, mostly unsigned, to such periodicals as *Vogue*, *The New Republic*, *The Forum*, the *New York Herald Tribune* and *The Listener*.[12] She, and soon Bloomsbury's other writers (Strachey, Desmond MacCarthy, Keynes), appeared to dominate certain sections of the journalistic marketplace, enjoying a privileged position. Her critical voice and judgement also became more confident, as in her critique of 1905 of Henry James's *The Golden Bowl*:

> We have been living with thoughts and emotions, not with live people. [James], with a sure knowledge of anatomy, paints every bone and muscle in the human frame; [but] the portrait would be greater as a work of art if he were content to say less and suggest more.[13]

A new gift for understatement and irony appeared. She also began to earn money regularly: in June 1906, for example, she received

Photograph of Lytton Strachey in the garden at Asheham House.

£9 7s for an essay on Wordsworth and the Lake District in the *TLS*; this was the largest amount she had made so far.

In 1905 Woolf began to teach once a week at Morley College, an evening institute in south London, and worked there until 1907. That year Thoby Stephen began the Thursday evenings at Gordon

Square, a gathering of his mostly Cambridge friends for discussion, debate and conversation. Clive Bell, for example, brought art into the mix and nearly twenty years after she had first met him, Woolf wrote that he still gave her great pleasure: 'for one thing because he says outright what I spend my life in concealing' (*LETT*, III, 79). Lytton Strachey, the eleventh child of Sir Richard Strachey, who spent thirty years in India as a soldier and public administrator, was also a bright star in this remarkable firmament of educated iconoclasts.

A cousin of Duncan Grant, Strachey became an intimate of Clive Bell, Thoby Stephen and Leonard Woolf at Cambridge and became a member of the Apostles in 1902 (a secret society founded in 1820), after going up to Cambridge in 1899. Strachey became Leonard Woolf's closest friend and frequently updated him on his love affairs. Strachey stood out, partly because of his unorthodox ideas, wit and originality, and he was echoed in the character of St John Hirst in *The Voyage Out*:

> 'D'you mean to tell me you've reached the age of twenty-four without reading Gibbon?' he demanded
> 'Yes, I have', she answered
> '*Mon Dieu!*' he exclaimed, throwing out his hands. 'You must begin tomorrow. I shall send you my copy . . . Have you got a mind, or are you like the rest of your sex? You seem to me absurdly young compared with women of your age.' (*VO*, 172)

Strachey withheld little, as evidenced by his revolutionary book *Eminent Victorians* (1918), which exposed the hypocrisy and inflated reputations of four prominent figures: Florence Nightingale, Cardinal Manning, Thomas Arnold and General Gordon. His sizing up of people's character was nowhere more evident than in his comment on the widow of the philosopher Henry Sidgwick, referring to her as 'a faded moonlight of ugly beauty with a nervous laugh and an infinitely remote mind, which mysteriously realises all'. Strachey had at times a 'slightly hysterical view of the world' and rebelled against cant and sexual oppression.[14] His biography of Queen Victoria (dedicated to Woolf) appeared in 1921 and *Elizabeth and Essex* – with its suggestions of androgyny that parallel *Orlando* – in 1928.

Strachey also had a passion for all things French, which would later translate into the Bloomsbury Group's culinary interest in French food and wine, especially from Côtes de Provence. Bloomsbury members, in fact, had an appetite for creative food, especially after the First World War. (*The Bloomsbury Cookbook* (2014) contains over 170 original Bloomsbury recipes.) In *A Room of One's Own*, Woolf wrote that 'a good dinner is of great importance to good talk. One cannot think well, love well, sleep well, if one has not dined well' (*rm*, 23). Food takes up most of Chapter One of *A Room of One's Own*, notably a description of a lengthy luncheon party at a college hall and then dinner. Favourite foods of the Bloomsbury set included crème brûlée, Woolf's favourite as a child, 'Trinity Cream', a crème brûlée introduced at Trinity College, Cambridge, often with the college's coat of arms burned onto the top layer of caramel (a favourite treat of Strachey's) and date palms, praised by Thoby Stephen. Thursday nights at 46 Gordon Square featured cocoa and biscuits on the sideboard – the cocoa perhaps because Roger Fry, who joined the group in 1910, was a direct descendant of the J. S. Fry chocolate family.[15]

Failing to achieve an academic career (such as a fellowship) – there is a well-known painting by Simon Bussy of Strachey from 1904, writing his unsuccessful thesis surrounded by books as he sits at a trestle table – Strachey became a man of letters, publishing extensively in *The Spectator* and *The Nation*. *Landmarks in French Literature* was his first book, published in 1912. His thinness and height and long red beard soon attracted attention and, despite various male admirers and adventures, he set up house with the painter Dora Carrington, thirteen years younger but his equal in rebellious spirit. Carrington's portrait of Strachey reading in 1916 conveys his louche but scholarly nature, although Strachey's hand holding a book is anatomically too large, but properly emphasizes his commitment to literature. Joining Carrington and Strachey at their second home, Ham Spray House, was Ralph Partridge, whom Carrington would marry – a second Bloomsbury *ménage à trois*; Vanessa, Clive Bell and Duncan Grant, with Duncan's lover David 'Bunny' Garnett, formed the first.

With Woolf, Strachey shared the tasks of a writer and she was often able to confide in him. They first met in 1901 when she visited her brother Thoby in Cambridge, and by 1905 he was a regular visitor to the Thursday evenings at 46 Gordon Square. Thoby, down from Cambridge, was reading for the Bar. Vanessa attributed the freedom of Bloomsbury talk to Strachey: 'his great honesty of mind and remorseless poking fun at any sham forced others to be honest too.'[16] Strachey also insisted the Thursday night group call each other by their first names, a small but radical anti-Victorian decision.

One could also talk freely at the gatherings; 'there was very little self-consciousness' – sex, art and religion were all openly discussed. And the term 'Bloomsbury'? Vanessa wrote that she thought Molly MacCarthy, Desmond MacCarthy's wife, first called it such to distinguish the group from Chelsea, where many of the so-called artistic 'highbrows' lived. Vanessa observed that Woolf was largely silent at the Gordon Square evenings, but when she and Adrian moved to Fitzroy Square in the spring of 1907, she participated much more vocally in the gatherings there because she was the hostess.[17] Precipitating the move of Woolf and Adrian was Vanessa's marriage to Clive Bell – the newlyweds would live alone at 46 Gordon Square.

Woolf and Strachey became close; he actually proposed marriage to her on 17 February 1909. Within 24 hours, however, he retracted his offer, both of them realizing that it was a mistake. Within another 24 hours, he wrote to Leonard Woolf in Ceylon telling him *he* must marry her. In June 1912 Strachey received a postcard which simply said 'Ha! Ha!', signed Virginia Stephen and Leonard Woolf. It was the announcement of their engagement and imminent marriage. That same month, Woolf wrote to Lady Robert Cecil, comically wondering why Leonard should marry her considering that 'he has ruled India, hung black men, and shot tigers', but 'he has written a novel; so have I: we both hope to publish them in the autumn. I am very very happy' (*LETT*, I, 504). A kind of rivalry developed between Strachey and Woolf, the former's celebrity status criticized by the latter. His *Elizabeth and Essex*, she felt, blended facile psychology with superficiality (*D*, III, 208). Nevertheless, as previously mentioned, she drew on Strachey's manner for her first novel, *The Voyage Out*, for the character of St John Hirst. Strachey read and praised the work when it appeared in 1915.

Creative work by others in the group now began to appear regularly: in 1905 E. M. Forster published *Where Angels Fear to Tread*. The privately printed *Euphrosyne: A Collection of Verse* was published with anonymous contributions from Clive Bell, Saxon Sydney-Turner, Lytton Strachey and Leonard Woolf. Works by established writers continued to appear in that same year: George Bernard Shaw published *Major Barbara*, as well as his play *Man and Superman*, while H. G. Wells saw *Kipps* in print. *Nostromo* by Joseph Conrad and *The Golden Bowl* by Henry James appeared the previous year, while 1906 saw *The King's English* by Henry and Francis Fowler, as well as John Galsworthy's *The Man of Property* (the first book in the *Forsyte Saga*), Rudyard Kipling's *Puck of Pook's Hill* and Edith Nesbit's *The Railway Children*.

The discipline of regular reviewing, mostly for the *TLS*, taught Woolf about deadlines, obligations and editorial responsibilities that would later help with her own writing and her partnering with Leonard at their Hogarth Press. Hermione Lee, in fact, suggests that Woolf's development into the type of novelist she wanted to be was 'worked out in large part through the essays of that period', ranging from reviews of individual writers to synthesizing studies of modern writing.[18] Not every review was a success, however: a piece on Edith Sichel's *Catherine de'Medici and the French Revolution* for the *TLS* was rejected largely because it seemed to offer too severe a criticism. From this and other rejections, notably from *The Academy & Literature* (her work was not adequately academic or contextualized), she learned to make her criticisms less abrupt and tailor her tone more to the ethos of each publication.[19] But as an antipathy to reviewing grew, her appreciation of the essay expanded. Literary journalism still held the key to her developing style; it soon came to dominate her fiction and, later, her autobiographical essays.

But Woolf soon found the distinction between reviewer and critic problematic. In her essay 'Reviewing' (1939), republished in *The Captain's Death Bed and Other Essays*, she tried to resolve it. Essentially, she believed the role of the reviewer was to 'sort current literature; partly to advertise the author; partly to inform the public'.[20] The critic, by contrast, was to deal with the past and literary principles. Nevertheless, much of Woolf's non-fiction writing was commissioned and often conditioned by space, editorial requirements and the nature of the individual periodical. Such writing, however, became the testing ground for her tone, style and ideas.

Bloomsbury soon encouraged a new sexual candour; Woolf wrote in her essay 'Old Bloomsbury' that 'the society of buggers has many advantages – if you are a woman.'[21] When Strachey burst in and pointed to a mark on Vanessa's dress and said in mixed company, 'Semen?', everything changed: 'We burst out laughing. With that one word all barriers of reticence and reserve went down . . . sex permeated our conversation.' A new openness emerged with frank discussion of the varieties of sexuality: 'we listened with rapt interest to the love affairs of the buggers . . . there was now nothing one could not say, nothing that one could not do.'[22] The old cliché that the Bloomsbury Group 'lived in squares but loved in triangles' may not have been inaccurate. The open acknowledgement of homosexual affairs was a social advance Woolf believed in, and in her work she broadened the link between private challenges to decorum and sexual conduct. The later openness of Vanessa's and Virginia's marriages – Vanessa's relationship with Duncan Grant even though she was married to Clive Bell; Virginia exploring lesbian sexuality with Vita Sackville-West while married to Leonard – reflects the liberal attitude of the Bloomsbury Group, as both sisters rejected the inhibiting and stifling social restrictions of the Victorian family.[23]

But if there was sex, there was also death. In the space of ten years, four close relatives had died. The sudden death of Thoby on 20 November 1906 from typhus following his return from Greece (he preceded Woolf, Vanessa and Violet Dickinson who went on to Constantinople) was as shocking as it was unexpected. When they returned to England on the Orient Express, they learned Thoby was ill, as was Violet Dickinson. Woolf and Adrian had to tend to both Thoby and Vanessa (who herself was not well) at 46 Gordon Square. Misdiagnosed with malaria, Thoby was found to have typhoid, but the diagnosis came too late. His death caused more grieving for Woolf, though this time she avoided a nervous breakdown. In fact, she managed to keep up a light tone in notes to Violet Dickinson while reporting on his condition, so as not to alarm her during her own illness. Woolf kept up this pretence that Thoby was getting better until mid-December, when Dickinson learned of it from a review of Maitland's just-published biography of Leslie Stephen. Woolf's facade had been exposed.

The death of Thoby haunted Woolf, as passages in her diary reveal. In one entry she wrote, 'How I suffer & no one knows how I suffer, walking up this street, engaged with my anguish, as I was after Thoby died – alone; fighting something alone' (*D*, III, 259–60). She would partly deal with Thoby's loss in two of her novels: *Jacob's Room*, where Jacob's death is unexpected (he, too, is a young

Cambridge man who dies aged 26, Thoby's age), and *The Waves*, where the character Percival, a kind of middle ground between the intellectual and the sportsman, dies in a horse accident in India. When she finished *The Waves* in February 1931, she offered another comment on the loss of her brother (*D*, IV, 10) and explained to her sister that 'I have a dumb rage still at his not being with us always' (*LETT*, IV, 391). Thoby's namesake, Julian Bell (Thoby's full name was Julian Thoby Prinsep Stephen), Vanessa's eldest child, similarly died young – in the Spanish Civil War in 1937, when he was 29 years old. Two days after Thoby's death in 1906, Vanessa agreed to marry Clive Bell, another of Thoby's friends.

Despite these losses, Woolf nonetheless found Gordon Square liberating and romantic, writing in 'Old Bloomsbury' that she was astonished to

> stand at the drawing room window and look into all those trees . . . instead of looking at old Mrs Redgrave washing her neck across the way. The light and the air after the rich red gloom of Hyde Park Gate were a revelation. Things one had never seen in the darkness there – Watts pictures, Dutch cabinets, blue china – shone out for the first time in the drawing room at Gordon Square . . . [but] what was even more exhilarating was the extraordinary increase of space.[24]

During this time, Woolf also began to attend concerts. Surrounded by music – Stella had played the piano and violin and there had been music at Hyde Park Gate and Talland House – Woolf often went to Queen's Hall to watch Henry Wood conduct. In February 1905 she attended the first performance of Strauss's *Symphonia Domestica*. That same month, she attended performances of Brahms and Beethoven at the Queen's Hall and saw Edward Elgar conduct his own music, including the *Pomp and Circumstance Marches*. She attended concerts regularly until her marriage in 1912. She

No. 46 Gordon Square, Bloomsbury.

From left, unknown man, Lady Ottoline Morrell, Virginia Woolf and Lytton Strachey at Peppard Cottage, Oxfordshire, 1910. Photographer unknown.

admitted that she had little musical talent but was inspired to understand more by Ethel Smyth, composer, feminist, memoirist and close friend.[25] Smyth met Woolf in 1930 and became a devoted, 'demanding, irresistible and intimate' friend (*D*, VI, 364). William Plomer, the South African writer published by the Hogarth Press, created an evocative portrait of their first meeting in his autobiography, noting that,

> The composer had a lot to say. The writer was almost immediately speechless because laughter, uncontrollable laughter, had taken possession of her . . . 'But Ethel –' she said, and got no further. Tears of laughter coursed down her face, while the composer, as sure of this good listener as of an orchestra in full cry, unswervingly pursued her theme.[26]

Expanding her social circle, Woolf met the independently minded Lady Ottoline Morrell in 1909, initially introduced through Strachey. Hostess, patroness, photographer, she was the most celebrated supporter of the arts of the day, and also made her Oxfordshire home, Garsington Manor House, a refuge for conscientious objectors during the First World War, men who were resident for supposed agricultural work and occasionally distracted by a flock of peacocks which roamed the garden. The first invited objector was D. H. Lawrence; Clive Bell and David Garnett, among others, were to follow. Ottoline's husband, Philip Morrell, was a Liberal MP.[27] She would regularly attend the second set of Thursday gatherings held at 29 Fitzroy Square, where 'long legged young men would sit . . . talking almost inaudibly in breathless voices of subjects that seemed to me thrilling and exciting'. Above it all could be heard 'Virginia's bell-like voice . . . awakening and scattering dull thought'.[28] Morrell mixed eccentricity with elegance and believed in action: 'Stagnation is what I fear; adventure and failure are far, far better', she claimed. At 1.83 metres (6 feet) tall (heightened by high heels and enormous hats), she became, in the words of Osbert Sitwell, 'an animated public monument'.[29]

As Woolf overcame a breakdown in 1915–16, she and Leonard went for their first weekend at Garsington Manor House, southeast of Oxford, with its swimming pool and peacocks. Leonard was smitten:

> Ottoline was herself not unlike one of her own peacocks, drifting about the house and terraces in strange brightly-coloured shawls and other floating garments, her unskilfully dyed red hair, her head tilted to the sky at the same angle as the birds' and her odd nasal voice and neighing laugh always seeming as if they might at any moment rise into one of those shattering calls of the peacocks . . .[30]

Painted by Augustus John and Simon Bussy, she was also the source of Lady Hermione Roddice in D. H. Lawrence's *Women in Love*; her theatrical manner drew welcome attention. She would become a lifelong friend of Woolf, who wrote her obituary for *The Times* when she died in 1938.

In April 1909 Woolf unexpectedly received a legacy of £2,500 on the death of her aunt, Caroline Emilia Stephen, Leslie's sister; by comparison, Adrian and Vanessa received only £100 each. Woolf had stayed with her aunt in Cambridge in 1904 when recovering from the breakdown following her father's death. A pious Quaker, Caroline Stephen idolized her brother, which irritated Woolf, who was aware of his shortcomings. Nevertheless, the legacy she received became mythologized in *A Room of One's Own* as one way to gain the security and privacy needed to write. Woolf wrote Caroline's obituary, emphasizing her aunt's accurate use of English and her intensely serious Quakerism. She was a possible source for Eleanor Pargiter in *The Years* and Mrs Swithin in *Between the Acts.*

Partly to overcome the devastating loss of Thoby and partly out of curiosity, Woolf began to explore London, often on foot and sometimes from the upper deck of a bus. Occasionally, if pressed for time, she would take the underground. Her fascination with the city, often hiking from the west to the east or walking along the Thames, found its way into her fiction, as Martin Pargiter illustrates in *The Years* when he pauses to admire St Paul's Cathedral:

He crossed over and stood with his back against a shop window looking up at the great dome. All the weights in his body seemed to shift. He had a curious sense of something moving in his body in harmony with the building. (*Y*, 216)

Parks, squares, neighbourhoods and streets form the fabric of Woolf's fiction, experienced by young and old. Jacob Flanders in *Jacob's Room* discusses architecture and jurisprudence in Hyde Park; Septimus Warren Smith in *Mrs Dalloway* hallucinates as he sits on a bench in Regent's Park. The city is not so much a backdrop as a character in her work, much the way it was in Dickens's writing. The city was similarly important in Woolf's own life: with John Maynard Keynes she gossiped in Gordon Square Garden, with Clive

Bell she talked about art in Green Park and with Aldous Huxley she discussed books in Kew Gardens. Place and space interacted with figures actual and imaginary to stimulate thought, imagination and emotion.

Oxford Street, for example, was a magnet that both attracted and repelled her, as her essay 'Oxford Street Tide' reveals. The buying and selling was 'too blatant and raucous' but as 'one saunters towards the sunset . . . the great rolling ribbon of Oxford Street has its fascination.'[31] Covent Garden similarly contains a clash of cultures, as Lady Lasswade experiences in her silver evening dress in *The Years*, as she is driven to the opera: as her car slows, 'Covent Garden porters, dingy little clerks in their ordinary working clothes, coarse-looking women in aprons stared in at her. The air smelt strongly of organs and bananas' (*Y*, 173).

The city excited Woolf but its mental effect and her nervous condition required her to spend time away in the country. Monk's House became a refuge from the excitement, tumult and stimulation. But Woolf understood that London was the source of much of her writing: 'London perpetually attracts, stimulates, gives me a play & a story & a poem without any trouble, save that of moving my legs through the streets' (*D*, III, 186). And after describing some of the pushing and shoving in the streets, she acknowledges that 'to walk alone through London is the greatest rest' (*D*, III, 298). Her fascination with Oxford Street, however, altered somewhat after she was robbed. In her diary from 23 December 1930, she recounts how she put her purse down under her coat and then in a flash it was gone, along with £6 and two brooches. 'Fluster, regret, humiliation, curiosity, something frustrated, foolish, something jarred by this underworld – a foggy evening – going home penniless', she wrote (*D*, III, 339–40). But London, as she emphasized in 'Street Haunting' (1927) and then in 'Portrait of a Londoner' (1931), is not merely a 'gorgeous spectacle, a mart, a court, a hive of industry, but a place where people meet and talk, laugh, marry, and die, paint, write and act, rule and legislate'.[32]

Walking and exploring should not, of course, have been unusual for Woolf, the daughter of an Alpinist, who told Vita Sackville-West in 1924 that she was brought up with 'alpenstocks in my nursery, and a raised map of the Alps, showing every peak my father had climbed' (*LETT*, III, 126). But London and the marshes, the city itself, were what she enjoyed best. As she wrote in 'Street Haunting', in stepping on to the street, 'we shed the self our friends know . . . and become part of that vast republican army of anonymous trampers, whose society is so agreeable after the solitude of one's room'. For her, a beautiful street in winter 'is at once revealed and obscured', the very mystery she pursues in her characters and fiction.[33]

3

29 Fitzroy Square, 1907–11

Think of a railway train: fifteen carriages for men who want to smoke.
Doesn't it make your blood boil? If I were a woman I'd blow someone's
brains out.

The Voyage Out (1915)

Vanessa's agreeing to marry Clive Bell two days after Thoby died
meant that Woolf and her brother Adrian had to move out of 46
Gordon Square. Displaced, they found a new home at 29 Fitzroy
Square, the southwest corner of a slightly decayed square where
offices, lodgings and small artisans' workshops had replaced great
houses. Vanessa and Clive Bell took over the house at Gordon
Square. In the 1890s, George Bernard Shaw had lived on the
second and third floors of 29 Fitzroy Square with his mother until
he married. In 1907 Woolf and Adrian arrived with their cook
Sophie Farrell, their maid Maud and a dog, Hans. Others soon
joined them: Duncan Grant had two rooms at 22 Fitzroy Square,
one to be occupied by John Maynard Keynes; Roger Fry started
his Omega Workshop at No. 33; Vanessa would later rent a studio
around the corner at No. 8 Fitzroy Street.

The drawing room on the first floor of No. 29 had G. F. Watts's
portrait of Leslie Stephen and a Dutch 'Portrait of a Lady' on the
walls.[1] Woolf had the entire second floor to herself with books filling
the untidy sitting room, which was dominated by a high table. She
would write standing up for two and half hours every morning,

View of the Georgian terraces at Fitzroy Square.

insulated from the sound outside by double panes. There she started work on *Melymbrosia* in 1907, which was completed in 1913 and published as *The Voyage Out* in 1915.

Guests would often arrive at 10 pm at 29 Fitzroy Square and regularly stay until two or three in the morning, surviving on a diet of whisky, buns and cocoa. Woolf, initially still shy, listened attentively, often addressing only those next to her, never the entire group, and smoking cigarettes she rolled herself into a long holder. Duncan Grant, who came regularly and was a great friend of Adrian's, referred to something 'a little aloof and even a little fierce in her manner to most men at the time'.[2] Yet the Cambridge group – Strachey, Keynes, Sydney-Turner, Bell – remained a constant presence and were welcomed and felt free to speak about anything before Woolf and her sister: 'Nothing was expected save complete frankness (of criticism) and a mutual respect for the point of view of each.' As Grant summarized of Woolf, 'no one so beautiful and so fierce could give offence except to the very stupid', but she could inspire feelings of respect in 'the most philistine'.[3]

Woolf could be harsh, Duncan Grant making that clear when he wrote that to be intimate with Virginia Stephen in those days was not to be on easy terms. Indeed the greater the intimacy, the greater the danger – the danger of sudden outbursts of scathing criticism . . . this shyness or fierceness was a necessary self-defence in her war with the world. The world must, she surmised, accept her on her own terms or not at all.[4]

Elizabeth Bowen, years later, recalled that Woolf 'could say things about people all in a flash, which remained with one. Fleetingly malicious, rather than outright cruel . . . anybody who bored her or anybody absurd she was often unfair to.' Woolf also eagerly wanted to know 'all the details of people's lives'. Angelica Garnett, her niece, referred to her combination of 'limpid beauty and demon's tongue', which 'proved fatal to those who were too timid to respond'.[5]

Woolf also liked to tease and draw people out and was physically 'economical in her gestures; yet she gave an impression of quivering nervous excitement, of a spirit balanced at a pitch of intensity impossible to sustain without collapse.' Even speaking was a performance; holding a cigarette, she would lean forward

before speaking and clear her throat with a motion like that of a noble bird of prey, then, as she spoke, excitement would suddenly come as she visualised what she was saying and her voice would crack, like a schoolboy's on a higher note. And in that cracked high note one felt all her humour and delight in life. Then she would throw herself back in her chair with a hoot of laughter, intensely amused by her own words.[6]

There was a playful side to Woolf; in 1909 for a fancy dress party at the Botanical Gardens, she dressed as Cleopatra. The following year she participated in the wildly successful Dreadnought Hoax, a plot orchestrated by Adrian and friends, including Woolf, to impersonate a delegation from Abyssinia asking to tour the navy's most secret warship, HMS *Dreadnought*. The retinue spoke a mixture of Swahili and whatever Latin they could remember. Woolf dressed in a turban and embroidered caftan, and had a gold chain hanging from her waist. The papers revealed the hoax, to the delight of their perpetrators, while also suggesting their anti-military stance – most of the Bloomsbury men would actually become conscientious objectors during the First World War. Woolf alludes to the incident in her short story 'A Society', in which a character tells of having visited one of Her Majesty's naval ships dressed as an Ethiopian prince. The cross-dressing anticipates some of the themes visited in *Orlando*.

Woolf also began to work informally for women's suffrage at this time, partly as a result of the influence of Janet Case, her early Greek instructor. A letter from 1 January 1910 to Case asks if she might help address envelopes for 'the Adult Suffragists' (*LETT*, I, 421). This

The Dreadnought Hoax, 7 February 1910, photograph taken at the Lafayette Studios just before the party set out by train to Weymouth. From left to right: Virginia Stephen, Duncan Grant, Horace Cole, Anthony Buxton (seated), Adrian Stephen and Guy Ridley.

was her early encounter with feminism, women's independence and freedom, and it would emerge in *The Voyage Out*. In the novel, Terence Hewet tells Rachel that he often walked the streets in London where people 'live all in a row . . . and wondered what on earth the women were doing inside' (*vo*, 245). He then expresses astonishment that it's the beginning of the twentieth century, 'and

Roger Fry, 28 February 1918, photograph by Augustus Charles Cooper.

until a few years ago no woman had ever come out by herself and said things at all' (*vo*, 245). That is all changing, he tells Rachel, and concludes with the vivid image of a railway train: 'fifteen carriages for men who want to smoke. Doesn't it make your blood boil? If I were a woman I'd blow someone's brains out', he tells her (*vo*, 245).

Woolf's more explicit remarks on women's suffrage occur in *Night and Day* and *The Years*. In the former, Mary Datchet works for an organization determined to secure the vote. In *The Years* Rose Pargiter attends a meeting that may be modelled on the Women's Social and Political Union in the '1910' chapter. In the next chapter, Rose is arrested for throwing a brick. Both *A Room of One's Own* and *Three Guineas* further document Woolf's expression of support for the struggle of women's rights, marked by her association with the Women's Cooperative Guild and the National Union of Women's Suffrage Societies.

A further addition to the Bloomsbury circle at this time was Roger Fry, the art critic and lecturer. Vanessa first met Fry at one of Desmond MacCarthy's parties in Chelsea. Clive Bell and Vanessa then ran into him one day in January 1910, on a train returning from Cambridge to London, and found him equally at home discussing Italian painting or Chinese art. Form was the product of feeling, Fry believed, and shape and colour generated emotion. He was also a painter and had studied studio painting at the Académie Julian in Paris, a few years after graduating from King's College, Cambridge, with a degree in natural sciences. He was introduced to Bloomsbury and spoke at Vanessa's 'Friday Club' at Gordon Square on 25 February 1910. Woolf attended and later recalled that he appeared 'in a large ulster coat, every pocket of which was stuffed with a book, a paint box or something intriguing . . . he had canvases under his arms; his hair flew; his eyes glowed.'[7] He was ten years older than most of the group and a Quaker who originally read science at Cambridge but rejected it for art. Woolf, in her biography of Fry, writes that he found it difficult to 'specialise', and instead

'Every week he was discussing "things in general" with the Apostles.'[8] Like the other members of the Bloomsbury Group, he refused to accept conventional ideas and always questioned received wisdom.

Fry had recently left the Metropolitan Museum of Art in New York where he was curator of paintings, helping the museum to form its collection. On his return, he declined the directorship of the Tate Gallery in hopes of the Slade professorship at Cambridge, but he did not receive it (in 1906 he had turned down the directorship of the National Gallery because he had agreed to go to New York). He became entirely dependent on his writing for an income. In London he also received confirmation that his wife Helen had to be institutionalized because of mental problems. His personal situation soon led to an affair with Vanessa, whose own marriage had reached a crisis point in 1911. His involvement with Vanessa brought him into closer contact with Woolf and he soon became a travel agent of sorts: he was responsible for the Bloomsbury set's travels to see Byzantine mosaics in Turkey and Italy, as well as taking the Bells to the studios of Matisse and Picasso.

In 1910 and 1912, Fry arranged for the first and second Post-Impressionist shows in England, both of which were controversial. The first introduced his aesthetic of colour dominating light and shade. With Desmond MacCarthy as his secretary for 'Manet and the Post-Impressionists', he exhibited modern foreign paintings (November 1910–January 1911). Fry and MacCarthy secured work from Paris dealers with such artists as Van Gogh, Gauguin, Manet, Matisse, Picasso and Cézanne represented. It was held at the Grafton Galleries in the autumn of 1912, and despite the hostility of the press and such viewers as Arthur Conan Doyle, who considered the painters rogues and charlatans, the paintings sold and nearly 400 people attended daily. For the second Post-Impressionist show, featuring works by British, French and Russian artists, Leonard Woolf became Fry's secretary.

Fry's aesthetic theory – that artists create rather than imitate form and that art is a means of communicating emotions as ends in themselves – emerged in 1908 and 1909 with 'Expression and Representation in the Graphic Arts' (1908) and 'An Essay in Aesthetics' (1909). He began to focus on design, mass, colour and significance. The impact of his ideas on Woolf was significant. As Fry turned to literature to understand painting – 'I have been attacking poetry to understand painting', he wrote in 1913 to his friend G. L. Dickinson[9] – Woolf turned to painting to understand literature. In 1917 she recorded a conversation in which Fry asked her if she based her 'writing upon texture or structure; I connected structure with plot, and therefore said "texture". Then we discussed the meaning of structure and texture in painting and writing' (*D*, I, 80). Later, his impact was noted in a letter she wrote to him in May 1927 complimenting him for his help in keeping her writing focused:

> you have I think kept me on the right path . . . I meant
> *nothing* by The Lighthouse. One has to have a central line
> down the middle of the book to hold the design together.
> I saw that all sorts of feeling would accrue to this, but I
> refused to think them out, and trusted that people would
> make it the deposit for their own emotions. (*LETT*, III, 385)

In the novel, Lily Briscoe completes her painting 'with all its greens and blues' with a single, calligraphic line down the middle of her canvas and thinks 'it is done' (*TL*, 170).

Fry's frank and at times brutal criticism of Woolf's work was actually a positive force. She considered him the most 'intelligent of my friends [who] was profusely, ridiculous, perpetually creative' (*LETT*, V, 366). He also boosted the confidence of Duncan Grant and Vanessa as painters. Fry, Grant and Bell were the first members of the Bloomsbury set to gain any measure of public recognition, around 1910–13. Woolf and Strachey had yet to make their mark.

Fry also started the Omega Workshops at 33 Fitzroy Square in 1913, devoted to decorative art relating to interior design, including furniture, textiles and hand-dyed dress material. It lasted on and off for six years, disrupted by the First World War. Part of his motive was to allow young artists to earn a living not only by the possible sale of their canvases but through interior decoration and designing tables, chairs, bowls, vases and boxes to harmonize with wall paintings, curtains and furnishings to create a total effect. Fabrics, furniture and pottery received special attention. The Omega design collective, founded by Fry (Duncan Grant and Vanessa were co-directors), generated no singular Omega style, although a preference for strong colours borrowed from the French Post-Impressionists dominated, along with a concern with the decorative arts. Photography was another element of the Omega impulse, the family albums and portraits of Grant and the Bells reflecting a concern with composition rather than focus and exposure. The event of taking a picture was considered more important than the processes involved.

But this was also a difficult time for Woolf, who had been unwell since March, partly because of her work and partly because of a flirtatious relationship with Clive Bell, her sister's husband. This began in 1908 following the birth of Julian Bell. Their entanglement brought on a powerful sense of guilt and feelings of abandonment by her sister, who had married Bell. The liaison may have been a means of getting back at her. But as their relationship cooled, Woolf later learned that he had renewed an affair with Annie Raven-Hill, also married. This went on during Bell's relationship with Woolf, and continued from 1909 to 1914. He later began a long affair with Mary Hutchinson, which lasted from 1915 to 1927, despite her having been married since 1910. But Bell still maintained at least the semblance of love for Woolf: just before her marriage to Leonard, he wrote that 'whatever happens, I shall always cheat myself in to believing that I appreciate and love you better than your husband does.'[10]

During their relationship, Woolf showed parts of *Melymbrosia* to Bell for comment. He had previously supported her decision to become a novelist but in the winter of 1909 objected to her portrait of men in the novel. Why were the women presented with such empathy but the men not?[11] To him, the men were all tyrannical, rude and ignorant, despite their education. She replied that as a man he could not judge properly how women viewed men. She continued to work on the manuscript through 1912, but never showed any more of it to Bell.

Woolf's illness may have originated in her blaming herself for Thoby's death: she did not act when she realized that Thoby's doctor was incompetent and misdiagnosed his illness. The doctor also advised Woolf not to get a second opinion and she agreed. Terence Hewet undergoes a similar crisis when he believes that Rachel's doctor in *Melymbrosia* (and in the more finished *The Voyage Out*) also errs. Rachel's death in both the first and finished drafts of *The Voyage Out* might be read as a symbolic substitute of her own death for that of Thoby. Further complications relate to Woolf's incipient affair with Bell. While on holiday with Bell and Vanessa, Woolf engaged in passionate debates with Bell on sexual differences and emotional if not physical attractiveness, all repeated or at least represented in *Melymbrosia*, which she was writing at this time.

While she was writing *Melymbrosia* the memories of her sexual abuse in 1888 at age six by her half-brother Gerald (and later as a teenager in 1904 when Gerald and his brother George likely pursued her) might have re-emerged. Depression or mental breakdown was likely a result of this proto- or incipient incest. Symptoms ranged from feelings of emotional coldness, detachment, mental anguish and negativity about her body, to disturbed sleep, food disorders, anxiety, fear and mistrust. Some of these features manifest themselves in her first heroine, Rachel Vinrace, who, like Woolf, was initially confined to the home by social custom and illness.

The triangular relationships in both *Melymbrosia* and *The Voyage Out*, between Helen Ambrose, Rachel Vinrace and Terence Hewet, echo Woolf's own difficult situation with her sister and Clive Bell. And in the novel, the married Richard Dalloway shockingly kisses the unmarried and vulnerable Rachel. In the first and even second versions of the novel, male behaviour dominates, Clarissa Dalloway responding to every demand of her husband and providing unquestioned support. Rachel, motherless, seeks help from other women such as Helen. At Santa Rosa, the two women meet Terence Hewet and his friend St John Hirst. Hewet tries to instruct Rachel and Hirst tries to command her. But Woolf essentially satirizes what the men supposedly know. Ridley Ambrose, for example, goes to South America to work on an edition of Pindar but can hardly find a proper chair to work in. The self-assured Richard Dalloway pontificates to Rachel on the weaknesses of women and their lack of logic.

Rachel and Terence form a relationship but she is repulsed by physical contact, telling him she has 'a wound in my heart'. Helen then pursues Rachel and falls on top of her, professing her love. Rachel is confused. After the trip upriver, however, Rachel becomes ill and dies. The journey by sea is a journey of the soul as it denies various temptations. The first draft also comments on the trade union movement, labour unrest and the suffragettes, plus additional social and political topics of the day. Woolf understood the challenge of presenting a woman who wanted to 'give voice to some of the perplexities of her sex, in plain English' (*LETT*, I, 381), as she wrote to Strachey in 1909. She continued to work on it throughout 1912 but chose not to publish it despite (or because of) its portrait of the effects of abuse upon the psyche of young woman and its critique of sexual politics.

Woolf would hide the manuscript when anyone entered her room, fearful perhaps that the ironic portraits of educated men would cause critics to dismiss it. After she recovered from the illness that followed the completion of a draft of *Melymbrosia* in 1910, she wrote two more complete drafts, finishing the one she chose to publish in 1912, after her marriage to Leonard, now retitled as *The Voyage Out*. It is less direct, with Rachel less angry and the politics and sex offered in a lower key. Textually, she cannibalized *Melymbrosia* for the finished novel, challenging critics to reassemble a reading text, which finally appeared in 2002. Woolf also made revisions for the American and English editions of the novel in 1920, deleting some 3,500 words and adding 728.[12] Customarily, Woolf destroyed the typescripts of her novels, saving only her holograph drafts, although *Melmybrosia*, which might be the ironic combination of the Greek words for honey and ambrosia, is an exception. The style of the work, however, borders on the excessive, as in this exchange between Rachel and Terence when he describes meeting her for the first time:

> 'The first thing I remember about you', said Terence, 'is your saying "Human Beings" at the picnic. I almost proposed to you on the spot.'
> 'Why?' she asked.
> 'You've a free soul!' he exclaimed. 'That's what I love you for. To you time will make no difference or marriage or anything else. We're both free. That's why our life together will be the most magnificent thing in the world!'[13]

In *The Voyage Out*, the tempered conversation focuses on context:

> 'When I first saw you', he began, 'I thought you were like a creature who lived all its life among pearls and old bones. Your hands were wet, d'you remember, and you never said a word until I gave you a bit of bread, and then you said "Human beings!"' (*vo*, 341)

The result of this intense reconstruction of these issues, even imaginatively, was Woolf's institutionalization at a nursing home in Twickenham for a rest cure in June 1910. Additionally, following the completion of the novel in 1913, she entered a prolonged period of depression and illness during which she attempted suicide, on 9 September 1913. Much later, in 1934, she experienced something similar, writing in her diary for 17 October that having finished a draft of *The Years* she was 'gloomy' and, looking over her past diaries, 'found the same misery after Waves. After Lighthouse I was I remember nearer suicide, seriously, than since 1913' (*D*, IV, 253). This came about in part because after the intensity of her creativity with her characters and their ideas, she was empty, a void, deepened by the absence, following their deaths in 1932 and 1934 respectively, of both Strachey and Fry.

4

38 Brunswick Square, 1911–15

In Jane Austen's *Emma*, Mr and Mrs John Knightley make their
residence in Brunswick Square. Woolf moved there with her brother
Adrian on 20 November 1911, shortly after attending a performance
of Diaghilev's radical Ballets Russes in their first London season. The
company would revolutionize ballet with its original choreography,
remarkable dancers and avant-garde music. Soon, John Maynard
Keynes, Duncan Grant and then Leonard Woolf would join them,
all living communally. Woolf and Adrian had decided to look for
a larger home after the lease expired at 29 Fitzroy Square. They
wanted a house to share with their friends and settled on No. 38
Brunswick Square. It was less noisy than Fitzroy Square and closer
to the City, where Woolf loved to walk. And living as the only woman
with four men suited her perfectly. Brunswick Square evidenced a
seemingly more radical social step than 46 Gordon Square or even
Fitzroy Square because by 1911 it seemed scandalous that a single,
unchaperoned woman would live in a home with four men, even if
one was her brother. Being 29 years old did not make any difference.
Following a letter from Woolf to Leonard outlining house rules and
dining hours, Leonard moved in to the top floor on 4 December and
he and Woolf soon renewed their shared passion for literature and
often took their meals together on trays in one of their rooms. She
even showed him pages from *Melymbrosia*. He almost immediately
fell in love with her and proposed three times before she finally
accepted, making him wait four months for an answer.

Grant and Keynes lived on the ground floor of the house, sharing a room decorated with a London street scene done by Grant. Woolf lived on the second floor in rooms with papers and books scattered about. Leonard, invited to join the group on his return from Ceylon, lived above her in what would have been the servants' rooms. But there were rules: breakfast at 9 am, lunch at 1 pm, tea at 4.30 pm and dinner at 8 pm. Trays were used, allowing people to dine separately, but they often joined each other to eat – although all trays had to be placed in the hall and returned with their dirty dishes. More than once individuals or the whole group went over to Gordon Square to dine with Vanessa and Clive when they tired of the tray system.[1] But visitors soon descended on 38 Brunswick Square as they had done at Gordon Square and Fitzroy Square.

In June 1911 Woolf wrote to Vanessa, depressed: 'to be 29 and unmarried – to be a failure – childless – insane too, no writer' (*LETT*, I, 466). Fourteen months later that would all change when she married Leonard Woolf on Saturday 9 August 1912 at St Pancras Town Hall. But not long after the ceremony, she would experience a third, severe mental breakdown, recounted later in a letter of 1930 to her friend Ethyl Smyth:

> And then I married, and then my brains went up in a shower of fireworks. As an experience, madness is terrific I can assure you, and not to be sniffed at; and in its lava I still find most of the things I write about. (*LETT*, IV, 180)

Woolf's interest in Leonard, as she writes to her friend Madge Vaughan, was initially in his 'governing natives, inventing ploughs, shooting tigers' (*LETT*, I, 503). He was also Jewish and writing his own novel, but, as she wrote to Violet Dickinson, he 'thinks my writing the best part of me' and he wants me to say 'that if I cease to write when married, I shall be divorced' (*LETT*, I, 502). Of course, Virginia had published much before her marriage – 69 critical essays

– but in her own words, written to Lytton Strachey in 1909, she was 'a painstaking woman', careful, meticulous and cautious, only at ease with those she thought intellectually her equal (*LETT*, I, 38).

Born in 1880 in London and able to attend Cambridge on a classics scholarship, Leonard Woolf, like Virginia Stephen, lost a parent at a young age. The fourth of ten children of an assimilated Jewish barrister and Queen's Counsel, his father died in 1892, when Leonard was eleven; Virginia lost her mother when she was thirteen. Sent to boarding school near Brighton, Leonard then went on to St Paul's School in London, where he was often the butt of anti-Semitic jibes. One of his classmates, the soon-to-be novelist Compton MacKenzie, based his character Emil Stern on the young Leonard. Stern was described as 'not yet developed enough physically to be called a handsome boy . . . A Gentile half as attractive would have won the glances of every ambitious young amorist in the school, but being a Jew he was disregarded.'[2] Leonard also inherited from his father a nervous tremor most noticeable in his hands.

In 1899 Leonard went up to Trinity College, where he was soon elected to the Cambridge Apostles, a group limited to twelve youthful, aspiring intellectuals. Other members included Lytton Strachey, John Maynard Keynes and E. M. Forster. Thoby Stephen was friendly with the Apostles, although not a member himself. Leonard met Virginia Stephen and her sister Vanessa for the first time in Thoby's rooms at Trinity during May Week in the summer term of 1903. Their white dresses, hats and parasols made a strong impression on him, despite their shyness.

Awarded a second-class degree in 1902 (earned as well by Strachey and Thoby Stephen), Leonard returned to Cambridge in the autumn of 1903 to study for the Civil Service examination. His exhibition money and scholarship had ended and he needed a career. He decided to sit the exam but had little preparation for the twelve examination papers, several of which were in areas he had never studied such as political economy and economic history. Despite his inexperience in the area, he was successful in the exam and in October 1904 he travelled to Ceylon (Sri Lanka) to become a cadet in the Ceylon Civil Service, first in Jaffna and later in Kandy. *Growing*, the second of his five-volume autobiography, narrates his adventures from the moment he stepped on board the ship which took him out.

Leonard remained in Ceylon from 1904 to 1911, a period that witnessed both the apogee and decline of imperial power, vividly narrated in his autobiography. He was a young intellectual and administrator who had had no similar experience. From the outset, he encountered unusual figures and situations but proved himself adept at confronting and solving human and bureaucratic problems. But, as summarized by one recent critic, he was 'a successful imperialist who increasingly became an anti-imperialist.'[3] In *Growing*, Leonard writes that he enjoyed the authority and the flattery his position granted him, although he claimed that he was unaware of entering 'Ceylon as an imperialist, one of the white rulers of our Asiatic Empire'.[4] He was, of course, fresh from Cambridge and only 24 years old. As time went on, his experiences led to ambivalence about his position and a realization that the system was actually exploitative and harmful. Despite his authority in the province of Kandy, he felt that the feudalism of the Kandyans seemed purer than the imperialism of the British. Yet he continued to conduct himself appropriately, hosting Empress Eugénie, Sir Hugh Clifford, the colonial secretary and acting governor of Ceylon, and others who journeyed to the Sinhalese temple of the tooth relic, a revered shrine. In Ceylon, Leonard found that it was Buddhism that appealed to him, perhaps because he understood it more as a philosophy than a theology. In the final part of his novel about Ceylon, *The Village in the Jungle* (1913), he presents this view of the religion as a guide to moral conduct but not interfering in the daily life of its believers or imposing belief in supernatural beings.

Vanessa Bell, *Leonard Woolf*, 1940, oil on canvas.

Leonard threw himself into his administrative work, was promoted to assistant government agent and in August 1908 was placed in charge of running his own district in southeast Ceylon, Hambantota Province, which covered approximately 2,589 square kilometres (1,000 square miles) and contained 100,000 people. Leonard taught himself Sinhalese and Tamil and travelled throughout his district, dealing with agriculture, justice,

Virginia Stephen and Leonard Woolf at the time of their engagement, 1912.

public health, road building, taxation and petty problems. He got to know the people of the area and the lives they led. He kept a detailed diary of his daily activities, published in 1963, drawing heavily on it when he came to write *The Village in the Jungle,* set in southeast Ceylon, on his return to England in 1911. A murder in the novel is similar to an incident which Leonard himself had to investigate,

with a corpse slowly swelling in the heat. There is also a trial in
the book which takes place in the very courtroom in Hambantota
where he himself sat as the magistrate. The novel is authentic in its
observations, but differs from other accounts because it is told from
the Sinhalese point of view, an unusual perspective to have chosen
for a book of 1913. Edwin Arnold, E. M. Forster's publisher, published
the work. Leonard said some years later that his experience of empire
made him a liberal and his later witnessing of poverty in the East
End of London made him a socialist. He would soon work with
the Cooperative movement, become a Fabian and write a book,
International Government (1916), which influenced the founders
of the League of Nations.

Leonard returned from Ceylon in June 1911 and re-met Virginia
Stephen in July after dinner at 46 Gordon Square. Also present
were Clive and Vanessa Bell and Duncan Grant.[5] Virginia Stephen
at this time was thought by those who knew her to be self-absorbed,
sensitive, but unusually observant of others. She was also quick,
playful and clever. Throughout that autumn, Leonard continued to
see her almost daily after she moved with Adrian to 38 Brunswick
Square in late November 1911, which Leonard had inspected with
them before they rented. On 4 December 1911, she invited him to
become their top-floor tenant.

Despite numerous marriage proposals (all quickly refused)
throughout her young adulthood, including offers from Lytton
Strachey, Sydney Waterlow and Walter Lamb, Virginia Stephen only
hesitated with Leonard Woolf, leaving him in a precarious position.
Vanessa, nevertheless, encouraged him, writing that 'you are the
only person I know whom I can imagine as her husband.'[6] In
February 1912, still unsure of her intentions – he had proposed to
her on 11 January – he requested a four-month extension of his leave
from the Civil Service for private reasons, while Virginia Stephen
entered Jane Thomas's nursing home in Twickenham for the third
time. The secretary of state for the colonies appropriately wanted

to know what Leonard's 'private reasons' were. He refused to explain either on paper or in an interview, having also received an ambivalent letter from Virginia Stephen on 1 May explaining her mixed feelings for him. Nevertheless, he was encouraged, although he had little choice but to resign.[7] His letter was finally accepted by the secretary of state on 7 May 1912. Importantly, he had decided not to return to Ceylon even if Woolf would not marry him, and to forgo his £650 annual salary: 'I personally did not like being a ruler of the ruled', he wrote in *Beginning Again*.[8] To Leonard's relief and joy, Woolf finally accepted his proposal three weeks later at Brunswick Square on 29 May 1912. They went rowing on the Thames to settle their emotions.

Woolf wavered because of the emotional and sexual involvement a partnership required, and she made this clear to Leonard on 1 May 1912:

> As I told you brutally the other day, I feel no physical
> attraction in you. There are moments – when you kissed
> me the other day was one – when I feel no more than
> a rock. And yet your caring for me as you do almost
> overwhelms me. It is so real, and so strange. (*LETT*, I, 496)

Woolf plainly had hesitations about marriage, as her letters make clear, and she did not disguise her feelings, as the letter above showed. In particular, she emphasizes that his being Jewish and 'foreign' puts her off, and that she is 'unstable', passing from 'hot to cold in an instant, without any reason'. But she believes he will make her happy, although she is also 'half afraid of myself'. The letter registers her love for him and wanting him to be with her 'always', but with uncertainty. And sexually she wants nothing, but if he can go on and let her 'find my own way', that would make her very happy. She enclosed a photo of herself in a tweed skirt, cardigan and floppy hat, gazing upwards (*LETT*, I, 496–7).

The honesty of her letter and identification of what would be problematic – Leonard's desire, Jewishness and her instability – speaks to the frankness of their relationship and what marriage would involve for a spinster of thirty and an ex-civil servant who hoped to make a living through his writing. But what appealed to her was the possibility of shaping a new kind of marriage premised on shared personal, literary and cultural goals. Her vacillating behaviour would soon find expression in *The Voyage Out* with Rachel and Terence, and in *Night and Day*, her second novel, in the struggle of Katharine and Ralph and the battle between intimacy and independence. Leonard, in his novel *The Wise Virgins*, written at this time, also echoes these concerns, especially in the relationship of Camilla, who wants the romantic part of life ('it's the voyage out that seems to me to matter') and Harry Davis, who is Jewish and responds to his status in English society with anger, telling Camilla that there is no life in her, 'no blood'; 'Your women are cold and leave one cold . . . you talk and you talk – no blood in you! You never *do* anything.'[9]

Woolf had an especially difficult time adjusting to Leonard's widowed mother, Marie, who lived in Putney and was not invited to their wedding. A visit to meet her was awkward and uncomfortable, Woolf telling Violet Dickinson that 'work and love and Jews in Putney take it out of one' (*LETT*, I, 502). Those attending the St Pancras Registry ceremony on 10 August 1912 were Vanessa and Clive Bell, Roger Fry, George and Gerald Duckworth, Aunt Mary Fisher, Duncan Grant, Saxon Sydney-Turner and the artist and architect Frederick Etchells. No one from Leonard's family attended.[10] Clive and Vanessa gave a luncheon in Gordon Square afterwards.

In the spring of 1912, preceding their engagement, there was the impact of the *Titanic* disaster on Woolf's conception of writing and on her re-writing of *The Voyage Out*. As discussed in the Introduction, she had attended the *Titanic* inquiry in London on its second day (3 May 1912) with Leonard at Scottish Hall, Buckingham Gate,

London, chaired by Lord Mersey (John C. Bigham), officially known as Wreck Commissioner. What she might have heard that day were testimonies from crew members and other survivors. The inquiry would last 38 days and call upon 97 witnesses. The final report was presented to Parliament on 30 July 1912. Highlighting the controversy surrounding the sinking, while the inquiry continued, was an article by George Bernard Shaw entitled 'Some Unmentioned Morals', published in the *Daily News and Leader* (14 May 1912), accusing England of face-saving and protecting national pride while unmasking the romanticizing of certain supposedly heroic actions. That very day, Thomas Hardy recited his evocative 'The Convergence of the Twain' on stage at Covent Garden during a special dramatic matinee in aid of the Titanic Relief Fund. Sir Arthur Conan Doyle soon challenged Shaw in print on 20 May, and the controversy over the actions of individuals continued, with Shaw replying on 22 May. Woolf would no doubt have followed these exchanges, as well as, perhaps, an article by Joseph Conrad in *The English Review* entitled 'Some Reflections on the Loss of the *Titanic*'.

A further backdrop to Woolf's decision to marry was likely her discovery of her sister Vanessa's affair with Roger Fry.[11] Again, social and sexual pressure was uncontained, while relations were unstable, overturning normal conventions. Acceptance of Leonard may have been a protest against uncertainty in the midst of the social and sexual tensions around her. Also marking their marriage is that they both completed their first novels before the ceremony: *Melymbrosia* for Woolf and *The Village in the Jungle* for Leonard.

After a night at Asheham House in Sussex and a week in England, Virginia and Leonard honeymooned in France, Spain and Italy for six weeks, leaving in mid-August and returning in early October. Woolf read *Crime and Punishment* on the trip, writing to Strachey that Dostoevsky was the greatest writer ever born. Leonard read Arnold Bennett's *Old Wives' Tale*. When they returned they stayed briefly at Brunswick Square and then took rooms at 13 Clifford's Inn between Chancery Lane and Fetter Lane, off Fleet Street, rooms Leonard described in his autobiography as 'incredibly ancient, also incredibly draughty and dirty' and often drizzled on by smut.[12] But they loved the district, especially the contrast between the silence of the weekend and the boisterousness of the week (in November 1941, after Woolf died, Leonard returned to Clifford's Inn where he took a flat; he had been bombed out of his Mecklenburgh Square home). In December 1912 the newlyweds found the area exciting and often dined at Ye Olde Cock tavern on Fleet Street, partly because of convenience and partly because Woolf could not yet cook. They enjoyed their part of the city, not far from the Strand, and missed it when, because of another nervous breakdown experienced by Woolf, they moved – at Leonard's urging – to the quieter surrounds of Richmond in October 1914, where they then stayed for nine years.

While still in London, Leonard went to work for Roger Fry as secretary of the second Post-Impressionist Exhibition at the Grafton Galleries (October 1912–January 1913). The show included work by Cézanne, Matisse and several Russian artists. Leonard was responsive to Fry's manifesto at the time, which was stated in the introduction to the catalogue of the show, asserting that artists 'do not seek to imitate form, but to create form; not to imitate life, but to find an equivalent for life'. Fry's manifesto, plus Clive Bell's *Art* (1914), would have an impact on Virginia's next novel, *Night and Day* (1919).

Leonard Woolf was certainly not 'a penniless Jew', as Virginia would occasionally and sarcastically describe him, most directly in a letter to Violet Dickinson shortly after their engagement: 'My Violet, I've got a confession to make. I'm going to marry Leonard Woolf. He's a penniless Jew. I'm more happy than anyone ever said was possible – but I insist upon your liking him too' (*LETT*, I, 500). But although Leonard had neither an inheritance, nor a heritage, he was self-created and mature and that likely appealed to her sense of independence. At the time of their marriage he had assets of £506 to invest (most of it the remainder of winning £690 in a sweepstake at the Calcutta Turf Club Melbourne Cup in 1908); she had £9,013 in inherited capital and an extra £300, a third of the sale of her father's second home in Emperor's Gate.[13] Her investments brought an income of almost £400 a year. As their expenses increased over the years, however, they needed to earn between £400 or £500 a year. According to Leonard their book earnings were insufficient until 1929. Virginia's medical expenses were extremely high and she was extremely anxious about money matters. Consequently, she had a constant drive to earn, often through her reviewing and criticism, while Leonard explained in his autobiography that he decided 'to stop writing novels and to see what I could earn by journalism'. Between 1916 and 1929, Woolf wrote up to 47 articles a year and never fewer than ten.[14] Leonard scrupulously kept the account books.

A rhythm soon defined their lives, as Leonard noted in a letter to Strachey in April 1913. Writing from Asheham, a small, isolated house Woolf leased with Vanessa in the Ouse valley, between Newhaven and Lewes in Sussex, he explained that 'in the morning we write 750 words each, in the afternoon we dig; between tea & dinner we write 500 words each.'[15] Virginia had been to Sussex several times; following her breakdown in the summer of 1910, her doctors recommended a quiet alternative to the homes she had previously retreated to. She began to favour country life strongly, as she wrote to her sister on Christmas Day, 1910, telling her 'I love looking out places on the map; already I have bought two guides, and planned several expeditions . . . one becomes so simple in the country – running out at all hours' (*LETT*, I, 443). Nevertheless, there were incidents. Supposedly during their first night together, Woolf became intensely upset and Leonard resigned himself to a 'white' marriage.[16] Writing to Strachey from Spain while on her honeymoon, Woolf reported that,

> several times the proper business of bed has been interrupted by mosquitoes . . . they always choose my left eye, Leonard's right

ear. Whatever position they chance to find us in. This does not sound to you a happy life, I know; but you see, that in between the crevices we stuff an enormous amount of exciting conversation – also literature. (*LETT*, II, 5)

Following the completion of *The Voyage Out* in July 1913, Woolf suffered acute feelings of paranoia, insomnia and an inability to eat. Her mental state rapidly declined; on 9 September 1913 she suffered a complete breakdown culminating in an overdose of the barbiturate Veronal (sleeping pills) at Brunswick Square. Quick action by Dr Geoffrey Keynes, brother of John Maynard Keynes, who happened to be staying in the house and who rushed with Leonard to a hospital to get a stomach pump, saved her, although she was unconscious for two days.[17] This was her second suicide attempt, the first having occurred in 1904. 'I am, like my father, "skinless": oversensitive and nervously irritable', she later wrote (*LETT*, V, 408).[18] Delusions and a refusal to eat preceded this major breakdown. Another event that no doubt upset her was Vanessa temporarily leaving Clive Bell for Duncan Grant in 1914.

By 1914, when they moved to Richmond, Woolf appeared to have fully recovered, although there would be another more severe break-down in 1915. Before this, in 1914, she refused to eat or sleep – signs of her depressive behaviour – but Leonard was able to care for her while encouraging her to garden or cook. When she was relatively well, Woolf took cooking classes at a school in Victoria; in a letter to Janet Case she reported that she distinguished herself by 'cooking my wedding ring into a suet pudding' (*LETT*, II, 55).[19] Much later, when they settled at Monk's House, Leonard would often do the cooking, but for now, Leonard, to quote Hermione Lee, 'made Virginia's illness one of his life's works. He studied her mind for nearly thirty years.'[20]

In late February 1915, while Leonard was negotiating the lease of Hogarth House, Woolf had her worst breakdown and exhibited intense manic behaviour. Leonard described it as a 'nightmare

Hogarth House, in Richmond.

world of frenzy, despair and violence'.[21] She spoke incoherently without stopping, often for hours, until she lost consciousness. When she spoke to Leonard, it was only with abuse. On 25 March she went into a nursing home while Leonard organized the move to Hogarth House. The next day, *The Voyage Out*, postponed from 1913 because of her mental state, was published. With the aid of four live-in nurses, she eventually recovered and by September 1915 returned to Asheham. Leonard realized that the connection between her madness and her writing was close and complex and that her mental condition most likely originated in 'a sense of some guilt'.[22]

But the city remained irresistible. In mid-February 1915, she and Leonard went up to London, he to visit the London Library, she to 'ramble about the West End, picking up clothes'. After her shopping and tea, she wandered 'down to Charing Cross in the dark, making up phrases & incidents to write about. Which is, I expect, the way one gets killed' (*D*, 1, 35). Her sense of the city, both its excitement and danger, had been the very origin of *The Voyage Out*, where departure and return to London frame the adventure.

The earlier drafts of *The Voyage Out* were written by a young woman not yet engaged, while the rewriting and completion was the work of a married woman whose honeymoon had just ended. Rachel Vinrace, 24 years old and raised by two aunts, lacked formal education and sought to avoid burying herself in a marriage. In Santa Marina in South America, however, she meets and falls in love with Terence Hewet, who aspires to be a novelist. She dies after a short river journey, possibly projecting Woolf's own ambivalence about engagement and marriage in the decade following the death of her father. In *Melymbrosia*, Rachel was more feminist in orientation and less fearful; in *The Voyage Out*, Woolf shifts her character and she is timid and sheltered.

A notable quality of *The Voyage Out* is the similarities it shows between the characters and actual people. Helen Ambrose, wife of the classics editor Ridley Ambrose, resembled both Woolf's mother and sister, Vanessa. Mrs Dalloway parallels Kitty Maxse, a good friend of Stella Duckworth's who became close to Vanessa after Stella's death. The daughter of a judge, Kitty had broken off an engagement to Lord Morpeth but later married the editor of the *National Review*, Leopold James Maxse. She died in 1922 from falling over a banister in her own home. Elegant and sophisticated, Kitty became a model for Clarissa Dalloway, who first appears in *The*

Voyage Out, as Woolf suggested to Vanessa in a letter (*LETT*, I, 349). Ridley Ambrose suggests Woolf's father, Leslie Stephen; St John Hirst echoes Lytton Strachey and Terence Hewet possibly Clive Bell.

Another important feature of *The Voyage Out* is the introduction of Shakespeare into Woolf's work. Mr Grice, the steward of the *Euphrosyne*, the ship taken to South America by all the principal characters, reads *The Tempest* and suggests a link between Rachel and Miranda; he also recites passages from the play for Mrs Dalloway. Shakespeare would appear frequently throughout Woolf's work, epitomized, perhaps, in Chapter Three of *A Room of One's Own*, where she postulates upon the existence of a sister for the playwright. In Woolf's second novel, *Night and Day*, characters compare Katharine to Rosalind from *As You Like It* and Mrs Hilbery hatches a plan to buy copies of Shakespeare to distribute to working-class men and open a playhouse in which she, Katharine and William would perform the plays (Chapter 24). Mrs Hilbery also returns to her London home at Cheyne Walk with flowers from Shakespeare's grave (Chapter 33), while Mrs Cosham is never without her pocket Shakespeare (Chapter Twelve). The celebration of love in the novel is akin to *Twelfth Night*. Mrs Hilbery in fact likens herself to Shakespeare's wise fool. In *Jacob's Room*, Woolf's next novel, Chapter Four opens with a reference to reading Shakespeare.

Shakespeare quickly became a watermark for Woolf, thematically and methodologically. She cites him repeatedly in *Night and Day* (1919) and then repeatedly in her work, with even Mr Ramsay in *To the Lighthouse* wondering how many Americans visit Shakespeare's house every year – and if Shakespeare never existed, 'would the world have differed much from what it is today' (*TL*, 37)? Woolf even transposes actual people into Shakespearean figures, telling Duncan Grant at one point that her sister, 'old Nessa', had become 'a Shakespeare character in my mind, so that I often put her into action for my amusement' (*LETT*, II, 145). In April 1922 she reports to Vanessa that at Monk's House she only writes and reads,

reads and writes, noting that she had just been reviewing 'Shakespeare, Joyce' (*LETT*, II, 520). In 1924, while writing *Mrs Dalloway*, Woolf read *King John* and planned to follow it with *Richard II*; in August that year she reviewed *A Midsummer Night's Dream*. In autumn 1925 she read *Hamlet* and in January 1926, *The Tempest*. *Mrs Dalloway* contains over fifteen references to Shakespeare, duplicated in *The Waves* and repeated in *Between the Acts*. A late letter to Ethyl Smyth dated 1 February 1941, during the Blitz, poignantly summarizes Woolf's absorption with the playwright:

> Did I tell you I'm reading the whole of English literature through? By the time I've reached Shakespeare the bombs will be falling. So I've arranged a very nice last scene: reading Shakespeare, having forgotten my gas mask. I shall fade far away, & quite forget . . . (*LETT*, VI, 466)

Equally important for Woolf is her realization that Shakespeare taught her how to be stylistically economical as well as insightful. He was able to reveal 'a whole character packed in a little phrase', she wrote in '*Twelfth Night* at the Old Vic'.[23] Where a novelist might take three volumes to expose a character, Shakespeare does it in a phrase. She notes this in April 1930, shortly after finishing episode nine of *The Waves*. For Woolf, a brief scene or an allusion often summarized an entire episode or relationship.

The critical reception of *The Voyage Out* was positive but sales were limited. By 1929 the novel had sold only 2,000 copies in the UK. Strachey praised the work for its wit and solidity, as well as 'the secular sense of it all – 18th century in its absence of folly, but with colour and amusement of modern life as well. Oh, it's very, very unvictorian.'[24] Woolf agreed that the 'conception' of the novel 'did not make itself felt'. What she wanted to do 'was to give the feeling of a vast tumult of life, as various and disorderly as possible, which should be cut short for a moment by the death, and go on again'. The difficulty was keeping any coherence while giving the characters enough detail to make them interesting. But, she confessed, 'one gets too much involved in details' (*LETT*, II, 82). The *TLS* praised the feminine spirit and wit in the work, 'with its alert scampering' from one point to another, also noting that social manners in the novel are 'amusingly satirized'. The powerful and surprising ending is 'intense' and one is 'desolated by a sense of the futility of life and forgets the failure of design'. The *Athenaeum* of 1 May 1915 was less generous, complaining of ungrammatical language and passages verging on coarseness, although it had some shrewd observations and welcomed frankness.[25]

Increasingly, Woolf's breakdowns upended her life; Leonard offering the following description of their onset:

> She talked almost without stopping for two or three days, paying no attention to anyone in the room or anything said to her ... Then gradually [her speech] became completely incoherent, a mere jumble of dissociated words.[26]

In full flight of madness, birds spoke to her in Greek, her dead mother reappeared, voices told her to do unexpected things and she refused nourishment. Leonard offers a wry summary of the difficulties, written years after these incidents: 'Quite apart from Virginia's madness, life in Hogarth House during the first six months of 1915 acquired a curious atmosphere of wild unreality.'[27]

In between her disorientations Woolf exhibited a growing interest and involvement in politics, contradicting Richard Dalloway's pronouncement in *The Voyage Out* that 'I never allow my wife to talk politics' (*VO*, 68); 'May I be in my grave before a woman has the right to vote in England!' he declares (*VO*, 42), an equally outrageous statement. These two expressions indicate how

Woolf satirizes male power as politics became more important to her as a route to gender equality. Leonard, of course, was the principal influence: he worked arduously for a variety of political causes and travelled across the country investigating labour conditions and organizational systems. Woolf often went with him. Before their marriage, she did not greet politics enthusiastically; the activist in the street did not appeal to her, despite her playing a marginal role in the suffragette movement. The politics of meaning for her had to do with the nature of political relationships between men and women and their status in society, a position outlined in *A Room of One's Own* and *Three Guineas*.

Ironically, although her writings seemed to be on the radical, more subversive side of women's rights and equality, her political views, shaped in part by and in reaction to, Leonard's, tended to veer between radical and conservative, engagement and distance. Her brief involvement with the suffragette cause is a good example. Her participation in the Votes for Women campaign in 1910 was short-lived, consisting of addressing envelopes and attendance at several mass meetings, the result of encouragement from her friend and Greek tutor Janet Case.[28] Case, some argue, was a moral and political corrective to Virginia's attraction to aestheticism in art.

Aware of the large demonstrations in London in 1908 and 1909 for the National Union of Women's Suffrage Societies, an organization of women's suffrage societies in the UK, Woolf, nevertheless, did not participate, even in the active environment of social criticism and political awareness in Bloomsbury in advance of the 1910 General Election. Rather than enthusiastically support the vote for women movement, she observed from the sidelines. She partly records her response to the suffragettes in her second and longest novel, *Night and Day* (1919), with scenes in a suffrage committee office (Chapters Six, Fourteen and Twenty) and the writing of such documents as 'Some Aspects of the Democratic State' (Chapter 21).

In November 1910, amid the controversy over the Post-Impressionist show organized by Roger Fry, she attended a mass meeting at the Royal Albert Hall, planned in protest against Asquith's delay in forwarding to a vote the Conciliation Bill to give about one million women the vote – but felt she was wasting her time. Marches by women continued while Asquith delayed. The impending war, however, soon drowned out the movement and it would not be until 1918 that votes for women over thirty would become law.

The world of agendas, policy making and committees did not appeal to Woolf, as is evident in the suffragette section of *Night and Day* with its caricature of the women's suffrage office. But it was an early introduction to politics, shown essentially to be alien and slightly unreal, echoed later in the character of Rose in *The Years*. *Three Guineas* also refers to the fight for the vote, although satire of the anti-suffragettes is the focus as she notes that 'the fight for the vote is still generally referred to in terms of sour deprecation.'[29] She also felt uncomfortable with the middle-class clamour for political equality and was not entirely comfortable in the company of Jewish feminists.

The clearest sign of Virginia's distanced acknowledgement of winning a partial vote for women in 1918 was her account of attending a 'Suffrage Rally' at Kingsway Hall with Leonard in March that year. Momentarily elated by the multitude, she quickly became disillusioned and 'finally bored & unable to listen to a word. In truth this meeting seemed to beat the waves in vain', she concluded (*D*, I, 125). Leonard, however, increasingly became a sounding board and opponent as Woolf's political identity evolved. In her diary, for example, she wrote that she wanted to argue with Leonard through the voice of Effie (an early name for Katharine Hilbery in *Night and Day*) against his writing a pamphlet on 'arbitration' (*D*, I, 22). She also identified Katharine with her sister Vanessa.

Woolf was unafraid of admiring and criticizing Leonard at the same time:

I don't follow these economic questions very easily, but Leonard seems to be able to read and write and talk to enthusiasts without turning a hair. His book seems to be a great success – the reviews all compare him with Kipling – but I can't see that he has the vanity of the true author – which is a serious reason against his being one. *I've* never met a writer who didn't nurse an enormous vanity, which at last made him unapproachable like Meredith whose letters I am reading – who seems to me as hard as an old crab at the bottom of the sea. (*LETT*, II, 23–4)

In the same letter she remarks that they want to have a baby but will not, because '6 months in the country or so is said to be necessary first' (*LETT*, II, 23). More importantly, they both understood that her mental state and physical health prevented it.

5

Hogarth House, 34 Paradise Road, Richmond, 1915–24

Think of a book as a very dangerous and exciting game, which it takes two to play at.

Virginia Woolf, 'How Should One Read a Book?'

Early in March 1915 the Woolfs moved to Hogarth House on Paradise Road, Richmond, and began the Hogarth Press. The move came at an unsettled period in their life, Woolf suffering again from depression. She began a diary in 1915 but it lasted only six weeks. And as was the case with each book that she wrote, when she finished she was in a state of extreme physical, mental and nervous exhaustion. In February 1915 there was another, more violent recurrence of the illness which this time lasted on and off until about 1917.

Leonard, anxious to find some hobby or occupation in which he and his wife could engage and which would serve as a relief from her writing, turned to printing. They were both interested as amateurs in the art of printing and in March 1917 purchased a small hand press, some old typefaces and the necessary tools and materials. Their first book, with a print run of 150 copies, was issued in July 1917, a 32-page pamphlet entitled *Two Stories* containing Woolf's 'The Mark on the Wall' and Leonard's 'Three Jews', with four woodcuts by Dora Carrington. Vanessa Bell designed their logo, a wolf's head. The title page bore the imprint 'Hogarth Press, Richmond 1917'. With this book, they inaugurated the Hogarth Press, which soon came to offer works by T. S. Eliot, Katherine

Mansfield and the first English-language translations of books by Gorky, Dostoevsky, Bunin, Tolstoy and Freud.

One of their earliest publications was Woolf's *Kew Gardens*. Appearing in 1919, again in an edition of 150 with ten unnumbered pages, this short story was quite popular, partly owing to a positive review in the *TLS* by Harold Child. He referred to it as 'a thing of original and therefore strange beauty with its own "atmosphere", its own vital force'.[1] Hand-set by the Woolfs with two woodcuts by Vanessa, it went through a second edition that same year. Set in the Royal Botanic Gardens at Kew, colour dominates the story, which substitutes a rhythmic narrative of confrontation among four couples in the gardens for the hurried pace of *The Voyage Out* or even *Night and Day*. The generally linear narrative incorporates some of the aesthetic ideas Woolf outlined a few months earlier in 'Modern Novels', better known in its republished form, 'Modern Fiction'. Katherine Mansfield, whom Woolf first met in 1916, may have contributed to the structure of 'Kew Gardens' and its leisurely rhythm, with its focus on a flowerbed to shape the whole. The story conveys not only the visual impression of the gardens themselves but the mood of the characters that haunt them.

In the years immediately following, the business of the press expanded rapidly. Additional equipment was installed at Hogarth House, though soon some of the printing work had to be handled by outside firms. But sixteen of the 32 books published during the years that the press was in Richmond (1917–24) were printed directly by the Woolfs.

Richmond became a calm centre of creativity for Woolf. During her first year there, Woolf revised *The Voyage Out*, wrote 'Kew Gardens', oversaw the production of *Monday and Tuesday* (1921), a collection of eight short stories including 'Kew Gardens', and worked on her second novel, *Night and Day*, as well as her third, *Jacob's Room*. *Mrs Dalloway* was also begun there, although the Woolfs had moved back to Bloomsbury by the time of its publication. As the reputation of the Hogarth Press grew, they had new opportunities and turned down some notable works, most remarkably James Joyce's *Ulysses* in 1918, which was eventually published in 1922 by Sylvia Beach's Shakespeare and Company. Woolf was unsympathetic to the style and to the naturalistic, as well as experimental, elements of the novel, having read the first four episodes. She told Roger Fry that

T. S. Eliot, Virginia Woolf and Vivienne Haigh-Wood, Eliot's first wife.

T. S. Eliot and Virginia Woolf, June 1924, photograph by Lady Ottoline Morrell.

it's interesting as an experiment; he leaves out the narrative, and tries to give the thoughts, but I don't know that he's got anything very interesting to say, and after all the p-ing of a dog isn't very different from the p-ing of a man. Three hundred pages of it might be boring. (*LETT*, II, 234)

The exterior of Charleston, East Sussex.

In 1923, however, they would publish 460 copies of *The Waste Land* by T. S. Eliot with a striking blue mottled cover. But Woolf had difficulty with the typography because of the rhythm and spacing of Eliot's lines. Indeed, the press was not always a pleasure, and the labour was often intense. In June 1923, her diary records her frustration after standing for hours with their assistant Marjorie Joad at a box of type to figure out texts when instead she could be 'adventuring among human beings' (*D*, II, 250). At one point in early July 1923, she wrote to her friend Barbara Bagenol that 'the Press is worse than 6 children at breast simultaneously'. She went on to explain that for a time she and Leonard lived apart, she in the printing room and he in the basement, meeting only for meals (*LETT*, III, 55).

While Richmond became their new focus, there was competition from Sussex. In 1916, at Woolf's suggestion, Vanessa and Clive Bell acquired Charleston, a large country home with land off the Lewes–Eastbourne road. Discovered by Leonard, it had enough land to farm with a pond and fruit trees. Duncan Grant and his friend David (Bunny) Garnett, as conscientious objectors, had to find paid farm work to qualify to be exempted from military service; a farmer named Hecks would employ both men, so Vanessa, Clive and Duncan leased Charleston in the summer of 1916. John Maynard Keynes, who would contribute to the rent and expenses of the

Angelica and Vanessa Bell in 1928.

house, began to visit in October. At the time, he worked for the Treasury Department as an adviser to the chancellor of the exchequer. After the war he continued to visit, becoming so close to the family that he became godfather to Vanessa and Duncan's daughter, Angelica.

Life at Charleston became somewhat helter-skelter, however: Duncan and Vanessa painted in each other's rooms all day, Keynes wrote on probability or the history of currency – he actually wrote his famous critique of the Treaty of Versailles, *The Economic Consequences of the Peace* (1919), there – Clive pretended to read Stendhal, while his mistress, Mary Hutchinson, wrote letters and the children fell into the pond. Luckily, Strachey added in his summary of Charleston, the atmosphere was always comic.[2]

Charleston quickly became a popular escape for the Woolfs, as well as other members of the Bloomsbury Group. Over time, more and more valuable art would appear there, one curious addition arriving in 1918. Keynes and the director of the National

Lytton Strachey and W. B. Yeats with unidentified man at 10 Gower Street, London, photograph by Ottoline Morrell, 1931.

From left: Duncan Grant, Angelica Bell and Roger Fry at Charleston, 1926.

Gallery, Sir Charles Holmes, had gone to Paris to the auction of
paintings collected by Degas. Despite the war and threats to the city,
the two went to acquire paintings for England's National Gallery.
The main competitor was the Louvre. Holmes chose or bid on
relatively minor works, leaving Keynes free to bid and acquire
a study by Ingres, two paintings by Delacroix and a still life by
Cézanne entitled *Pommes*. Keynes returned to England triumphant,

but upon reaching Swingates, the entrance to Charleston, he had too much luggage to carry so deposited the Cézanne in a hedge. Duncan Grant and David Garnett rushed down to the shrubbery to retrieve it when Keynes remembered to tell them sometime later. At the time, Vanessa wrote, Cézanne was seen only in black-and-white photographs in magazines with hardly any of his paintings on view in England. The purchase was a coup.[3]

But as more and more valuable paintings appeared at Charleston, various security measures were taken including, at the suggestion of the Lewes police, a large bicycle bell painted red, to be rung in case of a burglary. Additionally, the pictures were wired up so that, if disturbed, an alarm would or could go off at the Lewes police station. The best precaution, popular at the time, was to hang the paintings high, almost against the ceiling, making them barely visible. Called 'the policeman's hang', the idea was that they would remain out of reach of thieves, their height also making them difficult to secure. The result, however, meant nearly blank walls at eye level, with 'the masterpieces tilted against the ceiling'. The hall, as well as other rooms, reflected this bizarre method of protection, as Vanessa and Clive Bell's son, Quentin, recalled.[4]

During this period, Woolf wrote her longest novel, *Night and Day*, dedicated to Vanessa. A novel of manners, it focuses on five young couples struggling against the restrictions of a late nineteenth-century society caught between Victorian limitations and Edwardian liberality. It opens with its hero Katharine Hilbery pouring tea for her parents at their home in Cheyne Walk, Chelsea, and ends 34 chapters later with Katharine and her admirer Ralph Denham, lawyer and critic, embracing (after overcoming numerous obstacles and conflicts) and planning a future before Katharine re-enters the house.

Early drafts of the novel appeared in 1915, written in bed while Woolf underwent the so-called 'rest cure' for her breakdowns. The source of Katharine, earlier called 'Effie', was Vanessa; as Woolf told Janet Case: 'try thinking of Katharine as Vanessa, not me and suppose her concealing a passion for painting and forced to go into society by George [Duckworth]' (*LETT*, II, 400). Woolf believed *Night and Day* to be a more finished book than *The Voyage Out* but also a necessary step – a novel of fact – in freeing herself for her more experimental writing, which would begin with her next work, *Jacob's Room*. *Night and Day*, she wrote, taught her 'what to leave out: by putting it all in' (*LETT*, VI, 216) – although sometimes she got facts wrong. One reader wrote to point out that she had roses blooming in Lincolnshire in December. A more personal reason for writing this conventional novel was that she wanted to write a work centring on 'the things one doesn't say; what effect does that have? . . . I mean what is the reality of any feeling', she wrote (*LETT*, II, 400). But she was also uncertain and 'afraid of my own insanity', so that she wrote *Night and Day* to 'mainly to prove to my own satisfaction that I could keep entirely off that dangerous ground' (*LETT*, IV, 231).

Literature makes a sustained appearance in the novel, from Shakespeare and Fielding to Scott, Byron, Macaulay, Browning, George Eliot and Dostoevsky. This is a novel with a major character named Cassandra. The presence of the poet Richard Allardyce, the aspiring writer William Rodney, plus the attempted historical writing of Ralph Denham, reveal the directness of Woolf's incorporation of literary work and authors into her story. References to Sir Thomas Browne and Thomas De Quincey also supplement reworkings of various genres: biography (Mrs Hilbery is aiding in a work on her grandfather), drama (Rodney is writing a verse drama), essay writing (Mary works on 'Some Aspects of the Democratic State') and history (Ralph imagines an account of an English village from Anglo-Saxon times to the present).

An apparent influence in *Night and Day* was Henry James, not only in narrative method but via a Mr Fortescue, who appears (and acts) like James in Chapter One. Katharine also resembles Isabel Archer from *The Portrait of a Lady*. Another link is Mary Datchet, modelled on Margaret Llewelyn Davies, who was secretary of the

Women's Cooperative Guild. Another parallel is Mrs Hilbery, based on Anne Isabella Thackeray Ritchie. Lady Ritchie, in fact, read the manuscript before she died. Chapter Seven is a paraphrase of an incident in William Makepeace Thackeray's life. Leonard may be the model for Ralph Denham; Katharine's visit to the Denham family at Highgate may draw on Woolf's accounts of visiting Leonard's family in Putney. Like Ralph, Leonard came from a large Jewish family. The work may also be a commentary on Leonard's *The Wise Virgins*. And just as Katharine aids her mother with a biography of her grandfather, so Woolf helped F. W. Maitland with his account of her father. Complicated marriage plots, with engagements made and broken, and misunderstandings are widespread in the novel – again Jamesian in nature. Intellectual exchanges range from discussions of literature and politics to mathematics and social welfare. It is a novel that covers wide-ranging topics, much like *The Voyage Out* but with more characters at cross purposes in the pursuit of love, reflecting the outlooks of contrasting generations.

Reaction to the book was sympathetic but reserved, despite E. M. Forster's claim that it was 'a strictly formal and classical work' (*D*, I, 310). Katherine Mansfield offered the most critical comment in an *Athenaeum* review, stating that it was impossible not to compare the work to Jane Austen and that it was perhaps offering 'Austen up-to-date' (*D*, I, 314).[5] She criticized its static quality, written as if ignoring the fact that the First World War had ever happened, and how it projected a certain intellectual snobbery. More recent readers, however, suggest that the novel shows a society disintegrating and embodying 'the very conflicts of battle'.[6] But the traditional structure and even the story limited reception of the work, readers becoming impatient with an unjustifiable number of scenes and details. Familiar narrative formulas dominated, if not stagnated, the form. But if Woolf was writing about new social norms, she also wanted new narrative structures, although this did not happen until she confronted the story of her brother in *Jacob's Room*, where she felt greater freedom to experiment – perhaps the only strategy to confront a painful past, both imaginatively and indirectly. The same year that *Night and Day* appeared she published her essay 'Modern Fiction', her solution to the narrative problems she was facing but did not yet know how to execute.

In his autobiography, Leonard notes that they first met the New Zealand-born Katherine Mansfield at Garsington, the home of Lady Ottoline Morrell. Mansfield was living with John Middleton Murry and there 'was an atmosphere about them then of what I can only describe as the literary underworld'. There was also an air of conspiracy, he adds. He liked Mansfield but felt she did not like him. She had a 'masklike face and she, more than Murry, seemed to be perpetually on her guard against a world which she assumed to be hostile.'[7] Despite her critical review of *Night and Day*, Mansfield was polite and interested in Woolf when they met after the review appeared (*D*, II, 44–5). She came to spend a weekend with them at Asheham and was 'extraordinarily amusing', telling stories of her experiences as an actress, but always with a 'masklike' face. She was a serious writer with the gift of an 'intense realist, with a superb sense of ironic humour and fundamental cynicism'. She got 'enmeshed', however, in the 'sticky sentimentality' of Middleton Murry.[8] To see them together in their Hampstead home made one uncomfortable because she was always irritated with Murry and angered with Murry's brother, who lived with them.

Mansfield had praised *The Voyage Out* in July 1916, although dining with her and Murry in mid-January 1917 left an unsympathetic impression on Woolf, who considered Mansfield a rival as well as a literary peer. She became a 'queer balance of interest, amusement, & annoyance' (*D*, I, 243), but the two did sustain a friendship and her death in 1923 unnerved Woolf, who wrote a lengthy diary entry upon learning the news (*D*, II, 225–7). In it, Woolf stresses Mansfield's inscrutability but also a kind of certainty they shared about books and writing which seemed to Woolf 'durable': 'there are things

A youthful Katherine Mansfield, who went to England in 1903 for her education and returned to live in 1908. She died in 1923, aged 34.

Exterior of Monk's House, Rodmell, East Sussex.

about writing I think of and want to tell Katherine' (*D*, II, 227). Katherine's writing was the only work she was ever jealous of. Mansfield's short story *Prelude* was the second publication of the Hogarth Press (1918); Leonard and Virginia Woolf spent nine months printing and binding three hundred copies by hand.

In 1919 the Woolfs themselves settled in Sussex, buying Monk's House in Rodmell to be closer to Vanessa. It was a run-down eighteenth-century weatherboarded cottage without electricity or heat but with three-quarters of an acre of garden. Seventy-five kilometres (47 miles) from London, Rodmell had only a single street and 244 residents when the Woolfs moved there. It was almost 5 kilometres (3 miles) from Lewes in East Sussex. The house had a rural character with low ceilings and naked wood beams – when they bought the house water had to be drawn up from a well – and the Woolfs constantly sought to improve it, adding a two-storey extension in 1929. The previous year they bought an adjoining field to preserve the views. Between 1919 and 1940, the Woolfs undertook more than sixteen substantial enlargements and modernizations of the house and grounds. The first bathroom was installed in 1925–6 followed by electrification in 1931 and a telephone in 1932. The sizeable garden behind became Leonard Woolf's passion, while a wooden shed at the bottom of the garden was Woolf's writerly refuge; Woolf worked on all of her major books there.

Nevertheless, London continued to fascinate. On 8 June 1920, for example, Woolf had one of her 'field days', visiting the National Gallery with Clive, and having ices at Gunter's with 'much of a spectacle' around her as she observed a young man 'with a back like a clothes' horse hung with perfect grey clothes . . . [and] two young ladies with the mother eating in complete silence: not a spark of life, properly dressed', prompting her to ask, 'don't mothers & daughters ever talk' (*D*, II, 47)? She then dined with Vanessa and heard the full story of Vanessa's servant Mary and her hysteria, until she departed and had a vivid ride in the bright night on the top of a bus to Waterloo, where she saw an old, blind beggar woman singing:

Writing lodge, Monk's House, Rodmell, East Sussex.

there was a recklessness about her; much in the spirit of London. Defiant – almost gay, clasping her dog as if for warmth. How many Junes has she sat there, in the heart of London? How she came to be there, what scenes she can go through, I can't imagine. O damn it all, I say, why can't I know all that too? . . . Sometimes everything gets into the same mood; how to define this one I don't know – it was gay, & yet terrible & fearfully vivid. Nowadays I'm often overcome by London; even think of the dead who have walked in the city. (*D*, II, 47)

'The tension between standing apart and being fully involved; that is what makes a writer. That is where we begin', the Nobel Prize-winning South African writer Nadine Gordimer once wrote.[9] This applies clearly to Woolf, whose diary entries outline the anxiety and joy of writing.

The death of Thoby still troubled Woolf, and she would confront it in her next work, *Jacob's Room* – a work that would free her from the limitations of the traditional novel form. But she still experienced insecurity and a sense that no one was interested in her writing. In her diary for 8 April 1921 she writes that she should be working on *Jacob's Room* but cannot because she believes she is 'a failure as a writer. I'm out of fashion; old; shan't do any better' (*D*, II, 106). Her new book, *Monday or Tuesday* (published by the Hogarth Press in 1921), the only collection of her short stories published in her lifetime, would be out in a few days' time, but to her it was only 'a damp firework' (*D*, II, 106). Strachey's *Queen Victoria* (1921) – dedicated to Woolf – was now out and doing splendidly, which depressed her. She thought of never writing again, except for reviews; and Strachey failed to praise *her* new work, which upset her (*D*, II, 106). What if she was 'as plain as day & negligible?', she worried (*D*, II, 106). What really depressed her was 'the thought that I have ceased to interest people – at the very moment when, by the help of the press, I thought I was becoming more myself' (*D*, II, 107). She said she did not want 'an established reputation' as 'one of our leading female novelists' but to be interesting, not obsolete. To protect herself, she wrote that she should have a thousand interests such as 'Russian or Greek, or the press, or the garden, or people, or some activity disconnected with my own writing' (*D*, II, 107).

Working on *Jacob's Room*, however, provided the solution. In a letter to Mansfield from 13 February 1921, Woolf underscores their friendship and mutual commitment to writing. At the time, Woolf was writing *Jacob's Room* but had to break off from fiction writing to earn money for printing paper: 'I shall write an article on Dorothy Wordsworth and so pay for our new sheets.' In the letter, Woolf also contrasts her style to Mansfield's: 'What I admire in you so much is your transparent quality.' In *Jacob's Room*, 'I'm always chopping & changing from one level to another. I think what I'm at is to change the consciousness, & so to break up the awful stodge . . . I feel as if I didn't want just all realism any more – only thoughts & feelings – no cups & tables.'[10] In the novel there are 'chasms in the continuity of our ways' as 'frequent as street corners in Holborn . . . yet we keep straight on' (*JR*, 130). But not everyone valued this method; one reviewer likened it to 'snapshot photography [and] the result is a crowded album of little pictures'. The novel's lack of narrative, with its dissolving views swarming each other, reminds the reviewer of film, creating a work that itself seems to flicker.[11] Woolf herself published an essay on film in 1926 and Mansfield earned some extra money as a film extra. One technique of note was the dissolve, with one scene fading out as another fades in, showing both simultaneously, if only for a second or two. There is a hint of this in *Jacob's Room* when Woolf uses Mrs Flanders's letter to Jacob as an object parallel to the room used for his affair with a prostitute. The initial focus is on the letter but at the same time there are hints of action in the other spaces, the presence of the mother via the letter hovering over and around the illicit lovers (*JR*, 123–4).

Lytton Strachey, reading in Garsington Manor, 1922–3, photograph by Lady Ottoline Morrell.

Writing *Jacob's Room*, Woolf intended that 'one thing should open out of another – as in An Unwritten Novel – only not for 10 pages but 200 or so', and that there would be 'no scaffolding; scarcely a bride to be seen' (*LETT*, II, 13). This is evident in the second sentence of the novel, where the pale blue ink emanating from the gold nib of Mrs Flanders's pen dissolves the full stop so that her sentence flows from one into the next. Everywhere, words, scenes and ideas stream or blur into and overrun each other (*JR*, 3). Scenes are outlined not filled in, relationships intimated not developed. Whole paragraphs are repeated in new contexts; unexpected links recur to eliminate the need for sequential narrative. One part does not grow out of the other but stands adjacent to it. Discontinuities of chrono-logical sequences dominate. Connections are absent, embodying an aesthetic that Ezra Pound outlined in 'The Chinese Written Character as a Medium for Poetry', when he wrote that 'relations are more real and more important than the things which they relate.'[12]

Yet history is ever present, beginning in 1906 when Jacob goes up to Cambridge and also allusions to events before the cataclysmic First World War vie with references to the war itself, beginning with the Irish Home Rule Bill and the transformation of the House of Lords. Near the end of the book preparation for war becomes immediate as the ministers in Whitehall lift their pens to alter history (*JR*, 240–41). In the novel, there is only a single description of warfare, devastating in its implications. It begins with 'like blocks of tin soldiers the army covers the cornfield' and ends with 'one or two pieces still agitate up and down like fragments of broken match-stick.' 'Battleships ray out over the North Sea, keeping their stations accurately apart', introduces the scene of implied destruction (*JR*, 216).

The novel stresses colour and shape rather than incident, reinforcing its non-linear development as life is seen in flashes. The repeated colours suggest a form of unity but the fragmentary reigns, and readers, like characters in the novel, must piece together Jacob's life, having died in the First World War, although no description of his death emerges. Sorting out Jacob's possessions, the final task of his mother at the end of the novel, is also the task of the reader. But as the novel importantly reiterates and demonstrates, offering a kind of Woolfian aesthetic, 'it is no use trying to sum people up. One must follow hints, not exactly what is said, nor yet entirely what is done' (*JR*, 214). Woolf's method is to indicate rather than describe. The work also exhibits Woolf's belief that she and Vanessa were 'explorers, revolutionists, reformers', in art as well as life.[13]

Not everyone could follow 'the hints', however, and some criticized the novel. *The Guardian* claimed that it was 'one of the most arrogant books that has been written lately', while Rebecca West believed that Woolf preferred Jacob's room to his company and that the novel was no more than a portfolio of scenes, adding this memorable sentence: 'Mrs Woolf has again provided us with a demonstration that she is at once a negligible novelist and a supremely important writer.'[14] Furthermore, the novel is only about types, not individuals, wrote West. Woolf herself, however, felt satisfied. She understood her accomplishment and how the emphasis on simultaneity of action reflected the actual nature of lived experience. Following the completion of *Jacob's Room*, Woolf wrote on 26 July 1922 that she had found 'out how to begin (at 40) to say something in my own voice; & that interests me so that I feel I can go ahead without praise' (*D*, II, 186). But why the novel as her preferred form? In a letter to Gerald Brenan of 25 December 1922, Woolf explained that the form allowed her to move outside the limitations of one's own sensations. It permitted her to capture things that in the present were fugitive (*LETT*, II, 598).

The work and her growing confidence presaged her next three novels: *Mrs Dalloway*, *To the Lighthouse* and *The Waves*, all written in a six-year period. Anticipating her next work, *Mrs Dalloway*, is the love of London evident in *Jacob's Room*. Fanny Elmer's omnibus ride late in the novel responding to the congested streets and a

Vita Sackville-West, 1934, photograph by Howard Coster.

protest march, supplemented by reaction throughout Europe and beyond to the war, typifies what will dominate her next novel: the stimulation of urban life to live creatively (*JR*, 238–40).

Leonard interestingly described Woolf's writing practice as defined by intense concentration. She became part of the work and 'was absorbed into the novel'. She wrote only from 10 am to 1 pm and usually typed out what she had written by hand in the afternoon. But all day, whether walking through London or on the Sussex Downs or along the river Ouse, the book 'would be moving subconsciously in her mind' or she would be 'moving in a dreamlike way through the book'.[15] Such immersion made the writing mentally exhausting; Leonard, in fact, referred to her daily writing when completing *The Voyage Out* as 'a kind of tortured intensity'.[16] This hardly changed throughout her career.

Jacob's Room was the first of her novels published by the Hogarth Press, and Leonard found the book jacket for it unattractive, and wondered if it may have impeded sales:

> It was the first book with a jacket designed by Vanessa but it did not represent 'a desirable' female or even Jacob or his room, and it was what in 1923 many people would have called reproachfully post-impressionist. It was almost universally condemned by the booksellers and several of the buyers laughed at it.[17]

Nonetheless, Vanessa went on to design almost all of Woolf's later book jackets, alternating the style from formalized, geometric designs to elaborate set pieces of a representational nature. The clock on the mantelpiece for *A Room of One's Own* illustrates this. Her 'literal' covers, a lighthouse for *To the Lighthouse*, were generally impressionistic.

One other event of 1922 reinforces the year's importance for Woolf: meeting Vita Sackville-West, ten years younger and the wife of the diplomat Harold Nicolson. This was a pivotal relationship for Woolf, which had sexual as well as literary consequences. As one of the most privileged young women of the Edwardian era, Vita had grown up at Knole in Kent – a Tudor palace (supposedly the largest home in England) that had six acres of roof, seven courtyards and more than fifty staircases. Crawling through its hundreds of rooms

– there was supposedly one for every day of the year – was allegedly a pet tortoise with a monogram picked out on its shell with diamonds. At a London dinner party in the summer of 1910, Vita had met the young diplomat Harold Nicolson and immediately liked him, but only realized she loved him when he kissed her – two years into their courtship. But Vita lived an unorthodox and flexible romantic life: 'It never struck me as wrong that I should be more or less engaged to Harold, and at the same time very much in love with Rosamund [Grosvenor]', she later confessed.[18] Six years older and homosexual, Harold nonetheless fell in love with Vita, marrying her in 1913 at a ceremony in the chapel at Knole, attended by four duchesses and her father's secret mistress. The honeymoon period lasted for four-and-a-half years and produced two sons, Benedict and Nigel.

During this period, Vita published a volume of poetry and the couple appeared to settle down at Long Barn, a house they had bought in Kent. But soon her interest in a new relationship led to her involvement with Violet Trefusis (the daughter of Edward VII's supposed mistress), whom she ran off with to the remote village of Polperro in Cornwall. Unhappy, Harold wrote to his wife implying that he would drown himself in the Thames unless she returned. Disregarding his pleas, Vita and Violet travelled through France and Monte Carlo, where they stayed for four months. But the masculine disguise she adopted was not as successful as she imagined: at Monte Carlo they were forced to change hotels after a fracas when 'Julian' danced in public with Violet. To fund their bohemian adventures, the women relied on Vita's small private income and Violet's allowance – paid for by investments made for her mother, Mrs Keppel, on the instructions of Edward VII. Occasionally, the lovers had to pawn their jewels. Meanwhile, Harold had embarked on an affair with the diplomat Victor Cunard, and made sure Vita knew about it.

When Woolf first met Vita Sackville-West at Clive Bell's home on 14 December 1922, vaguely aware of her escapades, she wrote in her

Virginia Woolf and Vita Sackville-West at Monk's House, 1930s.

diary that Vita made her feel 'virgin, shy, & schoolgirlish' (*D*, ii, 217). Nevertheless, a relationship of some seventeen years soon developed, initiated in part by the Hogarth Press's publication of Vita's *Seducers in Ecuador* in October 1924; importantly, the source of their friendship was initially literary. This 74-page novella, dedicated to Woolf, undercut Vita's conventional romantic melodrama with irony, but

Woolf still offered writing advice. Indeed, over the years Woolf and the Hogarth Press 'tutored' Vita, who started to pay new attention to her craft.[19] Woolf would unhesitatingly offer criticism, telling her in one letter that 'I think there are odder, deeper, more angular thoughts in your mind than you have yet let come out' (*LETT*, III, 321). In September 1924, when Vita arrived at Monk's House to deliver the manuscript of *Seducers in Ecuador*, she entered with flair in a 'ringed yellow jersey, & large hat, & [with] a dressing case all full of silver & night gowns wrapped in tissue' (*D*, II, 313). Woolf read the manuscript quickly and sent it off to the printer a few days later, noting that in the story 'I see my own face in it, it's true' (*D*, I, 313). She also believed Vita had eliminated much of her old verbiage but still wrote to her that the manuscript could 'be tightened up, and aimed straighter'. She did, however, admire its texture (*LETT*, III, 131). The story had nothing to do with Ecuador or seducers but rather three strangers on a yacht in the Mediterranean, an impulsive marriage and euthanasia – the sensational mixes with the implausible. A strong review by Edwin Muir in the *Nation* and *Athenaeum* helped with sales and in approximately one month a total of 899 copies had been sold.

Over this period Vita charmed away Woolf's shyness, and at the end of 1925 the two became lovers. Of the two of them, Vita was initially the better-known and more commercially successful author, but it was the forty-year-old Woolf who had the reputation for cleverness as the author of 'high-brow' literature. In truth, Woolf considered Vita a second-rate writer, but she was intrigued by her 'full-breastedness' and realized that Vita 'may . . . have an eye on me, old though I am' (*D*, III, 52). What Woolf admitted was that the great appeal of Vita was not only her glamour and sexuality but something that had been missing from her life: 'she lavishes on me the maternal protection which, for some reason, is what I have always most wished from everyone' (*D*, III, 52). This telling remark addresses a gap in Woolf's life that opened with the death of her mother and had rarely been filled, except occasionally by her other, often older, female friendships – but not in the same way as with Vita.

Woolf had described female love before her encounter with Vita, expressing strong feelings for Violet Dickinson, who received passionate letters from the young writer. In *The Voyage Out*, Rachel Vinrace develops a powerful attachment to her friend and mentor Helen Ambrose. Katharine Hilbery and the suffragist Mary Datchet in *Night and Day* are also drawn together. Lily Briscoe is powerfully attracted to the maternal Mrs Ramsay in *To the Lighthouse.* Clarissa Dalloway momentarily feels desire for Sally Seton when she kisses her, and cannot forget the feeling. Lesbianism, as well as explorations of gender identity, appear in *Orlando*, topics which had been openly discussed in Bloomsbury. As Woolf wrote in *Orlando*, 'different though the sexes are, they intermix' (*OR*, 181). And through Orlando's gender change, Woolf contradicts Freud, who claimed that 'anatomy was destiny'. Woolf prefers the reverse: choosing one's sexual destiny is a triumph over anatomy; it untangles anatomy from destiny.

Vita made up her mind about Woolf quickly: 'I simply adore Virginia Woolf, and so would you', she told Harold. 'I've rarely taken such a fancy to anyone . . . I have quite lost my heart.'[20] Woolf was at first less impressed. In her diary she wrote: 'not much to my severer taste – florid, moustached, parakeet coloured, with all the supple ease of the aristocracy, but not the wit of the artist' (*D*, II, 216). Vita wrote straightforwardly to Virginia: 'I like you a fabulous lot.'[21] Woolf would write, 'Do you really love me? Much? Passionately not reasonably?' (*LETT*, III, 570). The two women soon began exchanging flirtatious letters – a correspondence that carried on for seventeen years, although their physical intimacy was of a much shorter duration.

December 1925 was the first time their relationship became physical. While Virginia was visiting Vita at Long Barn, something passionate ignited. Subsequently, in a letter, Vita referred to 'the explosion which happened on the sofa in my room here when you

Virginia Woolf in the 1930s.

behaved so disgracefully and acquired me for ever'.[22] Virginia described it as 'the night you were snared, that winter, at Long Barn' (*LETT*, III, 568), omitting to note that Leonard joined her and Vita for her third night there. Vita, however, was aware that a full-scale sexual awakening might put her new lover's fragile mental stability at risk. The following year Vita told Harold: 'I *have* gone to bed with her (twice), but that's all . . . I am scared to death of arousing physical feelings, because of the madness.'[23] Nevertheless, on 21 January 1926 Vita would tell Woolf, 'I am reduced to a thing that wants Virginia. I composed a beautiful letter to you in the sleepless nightmare hours of the night, and it has all gone: I just miss you, in a quite simple desperate human way.'[24] Almost exactly a year later, on 29 January 1927, she would write, 'Why aren't you with me? Oh, why? I do want you so frightfully.'[25]

Woolf's fascination with Vita may have been a fascination with illusion and the ability to make life 'vibrate' – Woolf's word. Woolf deeply felt her power and allure, playfully ordering her in 1927 to change her life:

> Look here Vita – throw over your man, and we'll go to
> Hampton Court and dine on the river together and walk
> in the garden in the moonlight and come home late and
> have a bottle of wine and get tipsy, and I'll tell you all
> the things I have in my head, millions, myriads – They
> won't stir by day, only by dark on the river. Think of that.
> Throw over your man, I say, and come. (*LETT*, III, 393)

Orlando, of course, would be the result of her strongest feelings, creating, as Vita would tell her, 'a new form of Narcissism, – I confess – I am in love with Orlando – this is a complication I had not foreseen' (*LETT*, III, 574).

6

52 Tavistock Square, 1924–39

Odd affinities she had with people she had never spoken to, some
woman in the street, some man behind a counter – even trees, or
barns.

Mrs Dalloway (1925)

Eager to return to London and life, and often restless and unsettled
at Monk's House, in 1924 the Woolfs moved to 52 Tavistock Square
and continued to operate the expanding Hogarth Press, now from
their basement. It was not always a pleasure, and as the press grew
it demanded more of their time, while Leonard wanted to devote his
energy to journalism, books and politics, and Woolf wanted more
time for her fiction. Mechanical tasks from typesetting (for shorter
works – longer works went to commercial printers) to packing
parcels and interviewing booksellers and salesmen took up time.
Although they had only two employees, an assistant and a secretary,
they needed to oversee the daily operations of a worrisome
enterprise – their net profit for 1927 was only £27.[1]

The Woolfs took a ten-year lease on the London property, which
Vanessa and Duncan Grant decorated, moving in on 15 March 1924.
The entire neighbourhood seemed to recreate Bloomsbury, with
Gordon Square, not far to the west, brimming with 'Bloomsberries',
as Woolf jokingly called them: Clive Bell had a flat at Adrian
Stephen's house at No. 50; Vanessa rented No. 37, which she shared
with Duncan Grant when not in Sussex or France; John Maynard

Keynes was at No. 46 with his wife Lydia Lopokova; Lytton Strachey's brother James was at No. 41, where Ralph Partridge also had a flat; and slightly further to the west Lady Ottoline Morrell had a residence at No. 10 Gower Street.[2]

The Woolfs rented only the basement and the top two floors at 52 Tavistock Square. The ground and first floors were leased to the solicitors Dollman & Pritchard. The set-up for the press consisted of a series of basement rooms once used as the kitchen, scullery and pantry, transformed into offices, a shop for booksellers' representatives, a printing room and storage space. A long dark passage connected these rooms to a large, skylit back room that had at one time been used for billiards, and which became Woolf's studio. Seated in an old armchair, with a board of three-ply on her lap,

Tavistock Square today with a bust of Virginia Woolf, erected by the Virginia Woolf Society in 2004.

Woolf regularly wrote for three hours a day when her health permitted.[3] After her writing, she would ascend the stairs, have lunch and work on a review, an essay or correspondence. From 4 pm onwards she generally entertained friends or ambled through the square with her dog.

During this time, she had been collecting as well as publishing her prose, which would soon come out in two volumes as *The Common Reader*. The first series appeared in 1925, dedicated to Lytton Strachey. During this time, she also worked on *Mrs Dalloway*, partly modelling Rezia, Septimus Warren Smith's Italian wife, on Lydia Lopokova, the Russian wife of Maynard Keynes. In May 1924, possibly reflecting her focus on psychology in the novel, Woolf and Leonard negotiated with the British Psychoanalytical Society over arrangements for publishing the International Psychoanalytical Library, leading to the English translation of the complete works of Freud.

Woolf in 1927, at Monk's House, photograph by Duncan Grant.

Exuberant London had now replaced dull Richmond: 'London thou art a jewel of jewels, & jasper of jocunditie', Woolf wrote in her diary (*D*, II, 283). But in July 1926 she experienced another nervous breakdown, which she referred to and titled in her diary as 'My own Brain'. Silent, unable to read, her mind became a blank: 'Character & idiosyncrasy as Virginia Woolf completely sunk out . . . thought I could write, but resisted, or found it impossible' (*D*, III, 103). Writing, for her, meant something alive: 'Once the mind gets hot it can't stop; I walk making up phrases; sit, contriving scenes; am in short in the thick of the greatest rapture known to me' (*D*, III, 161). Later she wrote, 'I used to make it up at such a rate that when I got pen & paper I was like a water bottle turned upside down' (*D*, III, 222). 'The only way I keep afloat', she explained, 'is by working . . . directly I stop working I feel that I am sinking down, down' (*D*, III, 235).

Nevertheless, several essays by Woolf during this period display her intermittent confidence as a writer, beginning in 1919 with 'Modern Novels', reprinted as 'Modern Fiction' in *The Common Reader* in 1925. Thomas Hardy and Joseph Conrad, she argues, outshine H. G. Wells, Arnold Bennett and John Galsworthy, who are no more than 'materialists'. Their concern with the body and not the spirit of their characters disappoints Woolf. They write of 'unimportant things' making the 'trivial and transitory appear the true and enduring'. Several paragraphs later, she famously writes that 'life is not a series of gig lamps symmetrically arranged; life is a luminous halo, a semi-transparent envelope surrounding us from the beginning of consciousness to the end.'[4] She concludes by citing James Joyce, who acknowledges that interior thought, as well as exterior action, defines character.

The first version of her essay 'Mr Bennett and Mrs Brown' (1923) and then 'Character in Fiction' (1924) would soon follow. Responding to Bennett's 'Is the Novel Decaying?', a defence of the realistic and traditional novelistic form published in *Cassell's Weekly* in March 1923, Woolf's 'Mr Bennett and Mrs Brown' challenges his assumptions as outdated. Strong emotion, felt first by the author and then the characters, is also a prerequisite for truth, the ultimate test of a successful novel, Bennett argues. He states that he has seldom read 'a cleverer book' than Woolf's third novel, *Jacob's Room*, 'which has made a great stir in a small world'. But he finds the characters unconvincing: the author 'has been obsessed by details of originality and cleverness'.[5] Woolf's response – partly to justify her treatment of figures in the novel – is to challenge the assumptions of character in Edwardian fiction. According to Woolf, Thackeray's *Pendennis* succeeded because of the vividness of physical character but the Edwardians changed tactics, focusing on social abuse and turning the novelist into a reformer. And then Dostoevsky revealed characters without features: 'we go down into them as we descend into some enormous cavern', she observes of Raskolnikov or Stavrogin.[6] Victorian individuality marked by convincing detail had been superseded by darkness, while the Edwardians concentrated only on generalities and types, an approach continued by the Georgians. Wells, Galsworthy and Bennett do not dig deep – Mrs Brown has no solid footing and changes in every scene she is a part of and the Georgians have failed to capture her.[7]

The second version of 'Mr Bennett and Mrs Brown' is more pointed. Delivered first as a lecture in Cambridge on 18 May 1924, it was then published in T. S. Eliot's *Criterion* with the title 'Character in Fiction' in July. It subsequently appeared as a pamphlet published in October 1924 by the Hogarth Press with its original title as volume one of *The Hogarth Essays: First Series*, with a cover by Vanessa of a woman reading. The essay is a stronger challenge to Bennett, and Woolf states that she wants to speak with 'greater boldness than discretion', arguing that 'on or about December 1910 human character changed.'[8] That year Edward VII died and the first Post-Impressionist exhibition was held. Human relations had shifted, she argues, which meant a change in religion, literature and the conduct of politics. For novelists, imparting character had become an obsession. She then narrates a story of a Mrs Brown and a Mr Smith in a railway car travelling from Richmond to Waterloo. Her anecdote, however, has no conclusion; her point is to make her audience understand how character can impress itself on another – in this case Woolf – although she intriguingly proposes differences if an English, French or Russian novelist were to write Mrs Brown's story.

But what is the reality the novelist is to present and who is to act as a model? Wells, Galsworthy and Bennett supply only incomplete examples. Sterne or Austen, however, were 'in things in themselves; interested in character in itself; in the book in itself', differing from the Edwardians.[9] Woolf imagines the three writers travelling with Mrs Brown in a railway carriage to Waterloo. Wells would disregard Mrs Brown and her travails; Galsworthy would rather spend time focusing on the upper class, while Bennett would indeed observe the details of the rail carriage (how the cushion would bulge between the buttons or how Mrs Brown mended her gloves) but hardly anything about her character, her feelings or emotions. Anything but the person is presented. Stressing only 'the fabric of things' and not the individual, for Woolf, actually destroys rather than creates character.[10] But the so-called 'Georgian' writers (she includes E. M. Forster, T. H. Lawrence, Conrad and Joyce here) have no tools to write the new, so they deconstruct what is before them: 'grammar is violated, syntax disintegrated'. Joyce, Eliot and Strachey lead the way. The job of the reader, then, is to demand that 'writers shall come down off their plinths and pedestals' to show Mrs Brown as a woman of infinite capacity – but until that is realized you must expect 'the spasmodic, the obscure, the fragmentary, the failure'.[11]

In addition to these essays and talks, in the summer of 1925, before *Mrs Dalloway* appeared, Woolf worked hard to complete several new stories and a set of reviews in an effort to earn £300 for a new bath and range for Monk's House.[12] She also acknowledged the value of publicity and was photographed by *Vogue* in April, the month before *Mrs Dalloway* appeared. When it did, it received mixed reviews: *The Observer* favoured it, as did E. M. Forster, but Vita Sackville-West was cautious – she preferred *The Common Reader*, calling *Mrs Dalloway* a 'will-o-the wisp', the very phrase Woolf had used in 'Character in Fiction'.[13]

In *Mrs Dalloway*, Woolf resurrected the characters of Clarissa and Richard Dalloway from *The Voyage Out*. Society, war and mental illness are among the topics addressed in the novel, as a statement from her diary outlined: 'I want to criticise the social system & to show it at work, at its most intense' (*D*, II, 248). The governing class is shown to be rigid and static, unable to deal with the trauma created by the First World War, which even medicine cannot overcome. The suicide of Septimus Warren Smith in the novel is a stark example of the inadequacy of a society frozen in its past and unable to confront the future. No direct war scene appears (in her later work *The Years* there is an air raid scene set in 1917), but its impact is felt almost everywhere in the text.

The novel grew out of a short story sequence entitled *Mrs Dalloway's Party*, more adequately understood as a series of preparatory sketches for the novel. The story closest to the novel is 'Mrs Dalloway in Bond Street', intended to be the first chapter of the book. Woolf was also writing 'The Prime Minister', a sketch that had a Septimus character plotting to assassinate the prime minister. She imagined incorporating both stories into a novel tentatively called 'At Home; or the Party', and began thinking of the novel after she had written *Jacob's Room*. In anticipation of the publication of *Jacob's Room*, she wrote in her diary: 'if they say all this is clever experiment, I shall produce Mrs Dalloway in Bond Street as the finished product' (*D*, II, 178). In 1922 when she made these remarks, she was reading volume two of Proust's *Remembrance of Things Past*, working on the essays that would appear in *The Common Reader* and re-reading Joyce's *Ulysses*.

The origin of *Mrs Dalloway* has many sources, not least Woolf's distrust of doctors experienced during the course of her own breakdowns. In the novel, Sir William Bradshaw and Dr Holmes are shown to be unhelpful and uncertain in their treatment of Septimus and his shell shock. Woolf herself had been given three different opinions on her condition and found them all unsatisfactory. The scenes depicting Septimus's madness may in fact reflect Woolf's own experiences in 1912–13. Several of his manifestations parallel Woolf's; for example, Septimus, mirroring Woolf's own experience, hears birds talk in Greek.[14]

The war, of course, is the great event in the novel, but except for Septimus it occurs offstage, and when and if it creeps onto the stage of the novel, figures react with unnatural stoicism. Clarissa idealizes Lady Bexborough, 'who opened a bazaar, they said, with the telegram in her hand, John, her favourite, killed'. The 'tapping of cricket bats' have replaced cannon fire (*MD*, 4). The worst that can be said about a 'nice boy' who was killed was that 'the old Manor House must go to a cousin', Mrs Foxcroft laments (*MD*, 4). Ironically, too many of Woolf's group assumed that the war was strictly a thing of the past and no longer a source of worry.

Counterbalancing this painful element of the story is Clarissa Dalloway's seemingly unscathed life in Westminster and her effort at party planning for her husband, a mid-level Tory politician. Her setting is posh Mayfair and Harley Street, where physicians treat the wealthiest in London. Clarissa, however, is being treated for severe depression and discovers that she cannot escape her past, as evidenced by the return of her early admirer Peter Walsh and memories of such moments as a kiss from Sally Seton, which still seizes her for its erotic intensity. The aftermath of Septimus's suicide while awaiting admission to an asylum, and Clarissa's realization that the past is very much alive for her, affects many. At the end of the book, it is Peter Walsh, processing the numerous changes in England since his absence in India, who asks – but cannot answer – 'What is this terror? What is this ecstasy?' (*MD*, 165). Woolf would spend her mature years attempting to answer these questions.

Politics is the indirect centre of the novel, not only with the appearance of the Conservative prime minister who arrives at Mrs Dalloway's party, but through Richard Dalloway's comments. Historically, it is a period of transition, with Labour about to replace the Conservatives led by Stanley Baldwin in January 1924, as several characters anticipate. Ramsay MacDonald would become prime minister, although he was in power for only a year. But Mrs Dalloway's class, politically and socially, was broadly under threat as the empire faced various pressures: in 1922 the Irish Free State was proclaimed, India was showing signs of restlessness under colonial rule and the governing party in England was unstable, making foreign relations difficult.

The world of the novel is also a world where the dead apparently return to haunt those in the present – or seem to. Peter Walsh, convinced Clarissa's aunt Helena Parry was dead, is shocked by her appearance at the party (*MD*, 151). Petrification rather than flexibility defines the society Woolf depicts, a society that will tolerate no disruption: 'what business had the Bradshaws to talk of death at her party?' Clarissa impatiently asks (*MD*, 156). The very idea of discussing Septimus's suicide is intolerable, although Dr Bradshaw mentions it to Richard Dalloway late in the novel in relation to a delayed parliamentary bill on the effects of shell shock (*MD*, 155).

Like *Ulysses,* the novel is set on a single day – a day in June 1923, linking several narratives in twelve unnumbered sections. But the structure is recursive, moving back and forth in time, providing a texture of consciousness that immediately pulls the reader in. Interestingly, in both *Mrs Dalloway* and Woolf's next novel, *To the Lighthouse*, elements culminate in a social gathering: the party in *Mrs Dalloway* and the dinner which is the conclusion of part one of *To the Lighthouse*. The assembly of people is an act revealing the collisions of character, shown internally and externally. What *Mrs Dalloway* shows is that the traditional forms of realistic fiction cannot contain the complex motivations and contradictions of either character or society. The novel exposes the play of memory, the effects of war, compromises in marriage, the gendered nature of the education system and the intricacies of politics, sex, religion and medicine. The new modernists at the time provided some direction: not only Proust, but Joyce. Woolf was reading *Ulysses* in August 1922 when she began an early version of *Mrs Dalloway*, which became, in her words, 'a study of insanity & suicide; the world seen by the sane & the insane side by side' (*D*, II, 207).

Reaction to the novel was varied, and Woolf wrote to friends to explain that she meant Septimus and Clarissa to be 'entirely dependent on each other' and that she wished Richard Dalloway to be liked and Hugh Whitbread 'to be hated' (*LETT*, III, 189, 195). Feeling that she had to defend elements of the novel, Woolf wrote a special preface to the work for the Modern Library edition, which appeared in the U.S. in 1928. Reviewers thought Septimus a distraction and that Peter Walsh was the dependant to Clarissa. But most critics felt it was her first mature work, one that centred life within the consciousnesses of her characters. The dual narratives of Clarissa and Septimus contest the novel's drive for unity but Woolf achieves it through psychological and thematic connections, creating one of her two most popular works (the other being *To the Lighthouse*). Ironically, Woolf herself was bewildered, as she told Janet Case, explaining that everyone seems to prefer either *Mrs Dalloway* or *The Common Reader* 'or the other way about, and implore me to write *only* novels or *only* criticism, and I want to do both' (*LETT*, III, 191).

Almost immediately after finishing *Mrs Dalloway* Woolf began *To the Lighthouse*, the idea for the novel occurring to her while walking in Tavistock Square, continuing a period of remarkable creativity. But while maintaining an active social and reviewing life – writing on *The Tale of Genji*, Jonathan Swift, William Congreve and Charles Dickens among others – she suffered a collapse. She continued with her work despite recurring headaches, even defending her technique. To Janet Case, who assumed that Woolf favoured method over thought, she replied: 'the better a thing is expressed, the more completely it is thought' (*LETT*, III, 201). She also read *Hamlet* in September 1925, attended the ballet at the beginning of December (her first night out in two months) and in mid-December began her affair with Vita Sackville-West, staying at Long Barn for the weekend.

Working on *To the Lighthouse*, however, was challenging. In a letter to Vita on 3 February 1926, she says she cannot maintain a social life while 'keeping my imaginary people going':

> Not that they are people: what one imagines, in a novel,
> is a world. Then, when one has imagined this world,
> suddenly people come in – but I don't know why one
> does it, or why it should alleviate the misery of life, and
> yet not make one exactly happy; for the strain is too great.
> Oh, to have done it, and be free. (*LETT*, III, 238–9)

Nevertheless she continued, recalling summers at Talland House at St Ives in Cornwall, where she visited on family holidays for thirteen summers, but which ended abruptly when her mother died in 1895. The family retreats to St Ives were a time of privilege, however, and the settling in from Kensington to the coast was a procedure that mixed labour with enjoyment and anticipation. Her parents participated in the community – Leslie Stephen a member of the Arts Club and her mother, Julia, pursuing work in public hygiene and nursing – and most evenings the children would watch the beam from the Godrevy Lighthouse sweep the sea. For *To the Lighthouse*, Woolf shifted the setting of her story from Cornwall to the Hebrides, reinforcing the idea of isolation by moving the action to the island of Skye off the northwest coast of Scotland.

Talland House, despite the warm memories it evoked, also held scars for Woolf, the most significant being Gerald Duckworth's sexual abuse, revealed in 'A Sketch of the Past':

I can remember the feel of his hand going under my clothes;
going firmly and steadily lower and lower. I remember how
I hoped that he would stop; how I stiffened and wriggled as
his hand approached my private parts. But it did not stop.[15]

A further challenge of the book was the image of her father and
mother. As initially conceived, Woolf imagined that 'the centre is
father's character, sitting in a boat, reciting "We perished, each alone,
while he crushes a dying mackerel"' (*D*, III, 18–19). When she finally
finished writing *To the Lighthouse*, she wrote that she 'ceased to be
obsessed by my mother. I no longer hear her voice; I do not see her.'[16]
The narrative priority of each parent remains in conflict in the text
but they are finally integrated by the completion of the book. The
novel is an elegy and exorcism of her parents: she was obsessed by
both of them 'unhealthily; & writing of them was a necessary act'
(*D*, III, 208). Woolf herself understood that she 'did for myself what
psycho-analysts do for their patients'. She expressed some 'long felt
and deeply felt emotion[s]', and in expressing them 'I explained it and
then laid it to rest.'[17] But in February 1927 she seemed to have doubts,
writing in her diary that 'if they – the respectables, my friends, advise
me against The Lighthouse, I shall write memoirs; have a plan already
to get historical manuscripts & write Lives of the Obscure: but why
do I pretend I should take advice?', she quickly adds (*D*, III, 129).

Lily Briscoe, as a reflection of Vanessa, is central in *To the
Lighthouse*, and the importance of the painting she works on
throughout and completes on the book's final page with a calligraphic line down its centre acknowledges Vanessa's own creativity
and aesthetic. Lily's abstract work, however, suggests rather than
describes Mrs Ramsay and James, which poses problems for the
painting's viewers, as Mr Bankes remarks. Mother and child are
'objects of universal veneration' but here they are rendered 'to a
purple shadow without irreverence'. Mr Bankes, as he taps the
canvas with the bone handle of his penknife, wonders what she

wished to 'indicate by the triangular purple shape, "just there?"'.
Lily replies that her work shows 'Mrs Ramsay reading to James' and,
defending her vision, tells him that 'the picture was not of them . . .
Or, not in his sense' (*TL*, 45). The dilemma of Mr Bankes is that of
the reader: how to interpret the abstracted characters? Are they
mirrors of Julia and Leslie Stephen or not? Are Mr Ramsay's egotism
and clumsy demands for emotional attention accurate or invented?
In a sense, it does not matter except in the fictional world of Woolf,
which remains artistically authentic.

What the reader must realize, as Lily understands, is that the
goal was 'not knowledge but unity' (*TL*, 44). Unity, in fact, is what
the novel strives for – something Mrs Ramsay experiences at
moments throughout the novel, including when she looks up from
her knitting to meet the third, long steady stroke of light from the
lighthouse as it reaches into her room: at that instant, 'it seemed to
her like her own eyes meeting her own eyes' (*TL*, 53). Matching this
unity of self, there is a unity of time as well as place. Hence the
timelessness of the lighthouse, but not the home, which decays
in the experimental 'Time Passes' section, the middle part of the
'H' diagram Woolf drew in her notebook outlining the shape of the
novel. The lighthouse – the desired goal of young James Ramsay –
is the guardian of ships and a symbol of man's attempt to control
the dangers of the world. Its steady light is a beacon and ideal, as
Mrs Ramsay is and, following 'Time Passes', was.

The third and final section of the novel is appropriately called
'The Lighthouse'. The novel's first, opening section is 'The Window',
offering a sense of looking out, looking forwards, looking beyond
the immediate. Coincidental with the final arrival of Mr Ramsay,
James and Cam at the lighthouse *and* Lily finishing her painting,
is the appearance of Mr Carmichael with a bouquet of violets and
asphodels, Mrs Ramsay's favourite flowers. As the flowers descend
slowly to the ground from his hand, Lily completes her painting:
the mythic natural world and the artistic world become one.

At the start of the novel, the eight Ramsay children are alive and active, whether it is six-year-old James (sixteen at the close), who in the final pages gains his father's long-sought-after approval, or Cam, their youngest daughter, who rushes across the lawn 'like a bird, bullet or arrow' (*TL*, 46), or Prue, who will die in childbirth. Death will also claim Andrew, who will be blown up in the trenches, likely dying instantly, and Mrs Ramsay, who is quietly, quickly, almost dismissively killed at the age of fifty. These tragedies happen offstage, often in parentheses.

In the novel, Woolf exposes the destructive power of men, which she would go on to challenge in *A Room of One's Own* and *Three Guineas*. At Charles Tansley's announcement that 'Women can't paint, women can't write', Lily becomes incensed and vows to prove him wrong (*TL*, 71, 74). The power of Mr Ramsay over his wife and children similarly supports the patriarchal authority in the novel, which lasts even at sea during the journey to the lighthouse. At the end, Lily assumes command of the land world through the completion of her painting, although Mr Ramsay, stepping grandly on to the lighthouse rock, still asserts his overall control.

Commenting on the psychological engagement with her parents in *To the Lighthouse*, Woolf would later write – using a nautical image – that 'I got down to my depths & made shapes square up' (*D*, III, 203). These ideas parallel those of Roger Fry: in his book *Vision and Design*, Fry explained that art does not 'seek to imitate form but to create form'.[18] Although 'the great plateful of blue water was before her' (*TL*, 14), as the narrator remarks of Mrs Ramsay early in the novel, Woolf finds ways to contain it (suggested by the plate) through art, family and self. Balancing the 'angular essences' of the novel is a kind of transformative poetics that mediates mass and form to make aesthetic perception possible (*TL*, 22). Natural objects and aesthetic configuration unite. The acts of writing and reading contain a bodily dimension that the novel fulfils both physically and artistically.

Woolf felt confident about *To the Lighthouse*, with advance sales totalling over 1,600 copies, more than twice the number for *Mrs Dalloway*. She presented a copy to Vita and it awaited her return from her second trip to Persia. Woolf inscribed it with: 'In my opinion the best novel I have ever written' (*LETT*, III, 372). It was a bound dummy copy with its pages blank – a joke. By contrast and in anticipation of success, Leonard ordered 3,000 copies to be printed and quickly requested a second impression of another 1,000 to follow.[19] Her fifth novel, *To the Lighthouse*, outsold all of Woolf's previous books – an achievement that allowed her and Leonard to buy a luxurious new car, a Singer, in July 1927.

Reviewed widely, *To the Lighthouse* was a success, with even the curmudgeonly Arnold Bennett admitting that it was Woolf's best work, although his compliment resounded with a schoolmasterly air: 'her character drawing has improved. Mrs Ramsay almost amounts to a complete person. Unfortunately, she goes and dies.' He thinks that the plot is too simple: 'A group of people plan to sail in a small boat to a lighthouse. At the end some of them reach the lighthouse in a small boat. That is the externality of the plot.' He then complains about Woolf's style, but grudgingly admits that the book 'has stuff in it strong enough to withstand quite a lot of adverse criticism'.[20] Others were more enthusiastic: Roger Fry told her it was the best thing she had done. Woolf's response to his remark on the potential symbolism of the lighthouse – 'I meant *nothing* by The Lighthouse' – contrasts with the comment that 'one has to have a central line down the middle of the book to hold the design together' (*LETT*, III, 385). In a review, the American poet Conrad Aiken noted how *To the Lighthouse* showed the change in Woolf's writing from the 'sterile dexterity' of *Jacob's Room* and *Mrs Dalloway* to something more powerful and affecting. In the new novel, Woolf had found the complexity to equal her technical skill. The use of stream of consciousness makes Mrs Ramsay 'amazingly alive' and Woolf achieves 'a poetic apprehension of life'. 'Nothing happens, in this houseful of odd nice people, and yet all of life happens', Aiken added.[21] Erich Auerbach, in his landmark book on literary criticism, *Mimesis,* cited *To the Lighthouse* in his final chapter to celebrate a new narrative method embodying the author's multi-personal attitude towards reality, with synthesis its aim.

Orlando appeared a year after *To the Lighthouse*. Published in October 1928, the new novel was a sensation; it was an immediate best-seller in Britain, making Woolf one of the best-known contemporary writers. As early as February 1927 she considered creating a work 'away from facts: free; yet concentrated; prose yet poetry; a novel & a play' (*D*, III, 128); she knew almost immediately it would be about Vita, who responded in October 1927 by writing 'My God, Virginia, if ever I was thrilled and terrified it is at the prospect of being projected into the shape of Orlando. What fun for you; what fun for me.'[22] Six days earlier, on 5 October, Woolf wrote in her diary that she imagined a biography 'beginning in the year 1500 and continuing to the present day, called Orlando: Vita; only with a change about from one sex to another' (*D*, III, 161). By 7 November 1928 she records that *Orlando* 'taught me how to write a direct sentence; taught me continuity & narrative & how to keep the realities at bay' (*D*, III, 203).

Written in the midst of a struggle to write a book on the nature of fiction, the idea for Orlando arrived unexpectedly. In a letter to Sackville-West on 9 October 1927, Woolf explained that 'as if automatically', amid her despair, she wrote on a clean sheet the words 'Orlando: A Biography'. 'No sooner had I done this than my body was flooded with rapture and my brain with ideas.'[23] Written with exuberance and energy, the result was a literary romp, a freewheeling literary history of England with a corresponding style for each episode. From the outset she conceived it as a satire, a fantasy, describing it in her diary as 'half laughing, half serious; with great splashes of exaggeration' (*D*, III, 168). Within a year of starting it, *Orlando* was published. Unlike the imaginative *To the*

Lighthouse, *Orlando* relied on history, 'facts' and real-life models, most importantly Vita Sackville-West. In her diary, Woolf noted how *Orlando* must 'balance between truth & fantasy', but that it is 'based on Vita, Violet Trefusis, Lord Lascelles, Knole &c' (*D*, III, 162).

But was *Orlando* a novel, a biography, a prose fiction or a prose fantasy? Booksellers placed it with biographies but Woolf objected, yet neither was she happy with the designation of 'novel'. By employing the narrative voice of a biographer she was able to achieve the 'firm, if rather narrow, ground of ascertained truth' (*OR*, 126). Nevertheless, the text, in Woolf's words, was 'potent in its own right . . . as if it had shoved everything aside to come into existence' (*D*, III, 168). But in fact she had been thinking of such a satire for some time, a work that would ridicule her own 'lyric vein' with 'everything mocked'. 'I need', she continued, 'an escapade after these serious poetic experimental books' (*D*, III, 131). The work, she wrote a few months later, 'should be truthful; but fantastic' (*D*, III, 157). She was 45 years old but eager to take a 'writer's holiday' from her other, more intense writings (*D*, III, 177).

Readers did not mind the fuzzy genre, or the exaggerations. For a character to be adopted by Queen Elizabeth, become England's ambassador to Constantinople and live among gypsies, in the eighteenth century choose to dress like a man, in the nineteenth undergo a sex change and become a poet and be honoured as such in the twentieth, seemed both fanciful and fun. The book was a best-seller, the public responding strongly to the history in the work and the avoidance of the psychological introspection that had been seen in *To the Lighthouse*. Yet among the parodic family history of *Orlando*, historical figures appear with regularity, from Queen Elizabeth I to Alexander Pope and Shakespeare. A two-and-a-half-page index, preceded by a preface and illustrations, enhances the appearance of textual reliability. The acknowledgements, fulsomely presented in the 'Preface', included Woolf's niece Angelica Bell, who posed in a fancy dress costume for the portrait of 'The Russian Princess as a Child', one of eight illustrations. However, there is no recognition of Vita Sackville-West, the dedicatee, or reference to her appearance in three photos representing the eighteenth, nineteenth and twentieth centuries. Embedded in the novel is Vita, from her travels in the East (the Turkish episode) to her transvestism (the sex change in the eighteenth century), her winning the Hawthornden Prize for 'The Land' (parodied by Orlando winning the 'Burdett Coutts Prize' for 'The Oak Tree') and her lawsuit over ownership of her home, Knole (the Great Law Suit). The events that make up Orlando's life echo that of Vita and her sexuality, and throughout the work Woolf revises and challenges ideas of sexuality and history.

The book opens in the Elizabethan period with the sixteen-year-old male Orlando and ends in 1928 with the publication of the book, Orlando now a woman. In six chapters relying on parody, pastiche and even burlesque to project its narrative, the work experiments with the conventions of biography. At one moment the narrator even names the date on which the passage we are reading is being written. Chronology is playful yet focused, even though the character escapes the effects of time. Orlando, sixteen when the book begins in the sixteenth century, is only 36 when it ends four hundred years later. Other characters similarly escape ageing, notably Orlando's housekeeper Mrs Grimsditch, who works for Orlando for two centuries, and Nick Greene, as he was called in the eighteenth century, but Sir Nicholas Greene when he reappears as a critic in the nineteenth (*OR*, 263–5). As the narrator writes near the end of the book, 'the true length of a person's life', no matter what the *Dictionary of National Biography* says, 'is always a matter of dispute' (*OR*, 291). The narrator also adds that 'nothing could be seen whole or read from start to finish', certainly in a world that seems to be entirely fluid and in flux (*OR*, 293). In such a situation the self becomes a multiplicity of identities able to call up other selves.

Orlando was a commercial and popular success in America as well as England; Britain's *Daily Chronicle* of November 1928 announced that 'the book in Bloomsbury is a joke, in Mayfair a necessity, and in America a classic.'[24] Following on from the strong sales of *To the Lighthouse*, the Woolfs became financially secure, even prosperous. The combined annual income of the Woolfs after *Orlando*, writes a historian of the Hogarth Press, was 'from two to six times as great as it had been in 1924'.[25]

While writing *Orlando*, Woolf was also struggling with a long essay, 'Phases of Fiction' (originally intended as a book), which she had actually started before *Orlando* but found tedious. Woolf eventually completed the work, which appeared in three parts in 1929, dividing novelists into various categories. The first category was 'Truth-Tellers', those who rely on a stable world, followed by 'Romantics'; 'Character-Mongers and Comedians'; 'The Psychologists', such as James, Proust and Dostoevsky; 'The Satirists and Fantastics'; 'The Poets', largely a comparative discussion of Sterne and Tolstoy, then Bronte and Meredith, before returning to Proust, who ends the discussion. While unable to conceptualize the novel as a whole, Woolf emphasizes that contemporary ideas of reality determine the nature of the genre, but that is a challenge as the novelist must simultaneously step back as well as provide a close-up of reality. Only a complete novelist can balance the two. Overly determined, the essay contrasts with *Orlando*, the former shutting out the reader with prescriptive categories, the latter providing open access for the common reader. The essay appeared first in *The Bookman* (New York) in the spring of 1929 and then in her posthumous essay collection *Granite and Rainbow* (1958).

In the same month as the publication of *Orlando*, Woolf gave the second of her two lectures at Cambridge entitled 'Women and Fiction', later combined with her first and published collectively as *A Room of One's Own* (1929). She also actively participated in the legal battles that censored Radclyffe Hall's lesbian novel, *The Well of Loneliness*, marking a concentrated period of attention to gender and sexual identity. That Orlando becomes a prize-winning female novelist in the contemporary period anticipates the argument Woolf presents in *A Room of One's Own* – that women can no longer be obscured or overlooked, and that they have genuine literary talent. The sexual shift in *Orlando* from he to she underscores the fluidity of gender and enforces the idea that success knows no gender barriers. In *Orlando*, this change, which occurs while Orlando is the ambassador to Turkey (in Chapter Three), is a highpoint in women's history, the text offering a new heroism for women who can and do succeed in the modern age, especially as writers, at least as defined in 1928 when the novel ends and where *A Room of One's Own* begins.

In many ways *A Room of One's Own* continues the allusive and widely referenced style of *Orlando*, although it is less directly fictional. While it eliminates the historical arc of *Orlando*, it nevertheless roots itself in another historical period: the sixteenth century, with its emphasis on the fictitious sister of Shakespeare. Among its remarkable connections is that Woolf first thought of such a talk at the funeral of Thomas Hardy in January 1928 (*D*, III, 173).

Woolf lectured in Cambridge first to the students at Newnham College and then, a week later, at Girton College. In the published text (the texts of the original talks do not survive), she emphasizes the importance of women finding their careers without or beyond the strictures of men and male institutions. Her trope is a 'Mary Beton' visiting 'Oxbridge' to give a lecture on women and fiction, but she is also the aunt in the text whose legacy makes it possible for the financial independence of the narrator. Ordered by a beadle to get off a college lawn and stay on the gravel path, and refused entry to the university library to examine 'Lycidas' or Thackeray's *Henry Esmond*, the narrator responds to these rules as institutionalized insults. In a manner that integrates the narrative style of a novel while asking critical questions of the status of women, Woolf succeeds at outlining a position that offers women direction and purpose. A 'room of one's own' quickly became a metaphor for independence of both thought and action.

Throughout the essay, Woolf confronts the problem of truth and illusion, initially connected to the First World War and the death of romance. This remains a constant theme even when she discusses Shakespeare's imaginary sister (Judith) and suggests that what she is outlining may be either true or false. What is true, however, is that any woman 'born with a great gift in the sixteenth century would have certainly gone crazed' because of restrictions, limitations and social conventions (*RM*, 60). Anon, she believes, 'who wrote so many beautiful poems without signing them, was often a woman' (*RM*, 59), and women must now resist anonymity.

But as Woolf also recognizes, women faced material as well as psychological challenges. There were virtually no circumstances that allowed them to develop their imaginations, certainly not in private. For women to be actors, writers or musicians had been not only difficult but likely impossible from the Renaissance until the present day. And it was not that women were treated as inferior; it was that men were simply considered superior. Women, especially if they aspired to be artists, were 'snubbed, slapped, lectured and exhorted' (*RM*, 67).

One of the more critical points in the essay is on integrity and the truth of fiction. Woolf acknowledges that books survive and are re-read because of their integrity, which is the conviction that what you are reading is the truth (*RM*, 86). But novels do come 'to grief' when the 'imagination falters' under the strain of composition and insight can no longer distinguish between truth and falsehood. Might not the fact of gender 'interfere with the integrity of a woman novelist' she asks, with integrity the backbone of every writer (*RM*, 87)? She then celebrates Emily Brontë and Jane Austen as women, not as men or women trying to write like men (*RM*, 89). This underscores Woolf's commitment to freedom as a core value

Virginia Woolf at Monk's House, 1927.

for women. Moreover, in commenting on the sentence styles
of men and women, she emphasizes that 'a book is not made
of sentences laid end to end, but of sentences built, if an image
helps, into arcades or domes.' What is important is that the 'book
has somehow to be adapted to the body' (*RM*, 92, 93).

In the sixth and final chapter of the essay, Woolf notes that by convention she should end with a peroration of some sort. But she doesn't really have one other than to be oneself (*RM*, 130). She is surprised by her own prosaicness but that seems to her more honest than any exultation, which would be false. She also admits that she likes the unconventionality and originality of women. Be educated, be strong, be vigilant and use the advantages you have, such as the vote, which was finally granted to women – though only to married women over thirty – in 1918, and then changed in 1928 to allow all women over 21 years old the right to vote. If the women in the lecture hall and beyond each have 'rooms of our own . . . if we have the habit of freedom and the courage to write exactly what we think', there *will* be change (*RM*, 133). However, one must acknowledge that one goes it alone and realize that 'our relation is to the world of reality and not only to the world of men and women.' Only then will Shakespeare's sister reappear and find it possible to live – and write her poetry – 'if we worked for her'; 'So to work, even in poverty and obscurity, is [then] worth while', she concludes (*RM*, 134).

Reaction to *A Room of One's Own* was as one might expect: Arnold Bennett believed Woolf was the victim of her own fancy, not imagination – fancy being a whimsical fairy-tale-like creation, while the imagination was a substantial thinking in logical but creative ways. The *TLS* welcomed it as a 'peripatetic essay', while Vita Sackville-West was surprisingly critical, arguing that Woolf was 'too sensible to be a thorough-going feminist'. Its so-called consciousness of sex affected its reception, Rebecca West celebrating it as an 'uncompromising piece of feminist propaganda' – the best yet written.[26] In subsequent years the volume, with its mix of literary criticism and feminist theory, has become one of the most celebrated works of the modern period. Contemporary critics and readers have repeatedly praised, as well as debated, the political and psychological aspects of the text and Woolf's understanding of the issues.

A few years after the publication of *A Room of One's Own*, in 1931, came *The Waves,* a structural experiment with an overlapping stream-of-consciousness narrative with six competing interior monologues. Leonard thought it a masterpiece, the best of her books, and E. M. Forster called it an extraordinary achievement (*D*, IV, 36).[27] Others, beginning with Woolf herself, had doubts: was there 'some falsity of method . . . something tricky', she wondered? 'Here's my interesting thing; & there's no quite solid table on which to put it' she remarked (*D*, III, 264). Earlier, in 'The Narrow Bridge of Art' (1927), Woolf claimed that the novel would take over some of the duties of poetry. The novel would give not only people's relations to each other but 'the relation of the mind to general ideas and its soliloquy in solitude.'[28] This echoes Terence Hewet in *The Voyage Out*, who wants to write a novel about silence, 'the things people don't say. But the difficulty is immense' (*VO*, 249). *The Waves* enacts the Woolfian dictum that thought is more important than speech. While Bernard identifies himself as only a maker of phrases, he also recognizes that he is 'not one person; I am many people', and so absorbs the thoughts, if not ideas, of the others (*W*, 231, 230).

Each section of the novel begins with a lyrical narrative passage describing the movement of the sun, one of the few markers of time in the work. The second of seven interludes begins,

> *The sun rose higher. Blue waves, green waves swept a quick*
> *fan over the beach, circling the spike of sea-holly and leaving*
> *shallow pools of light here and there on the sand. A faint black*
> *rim was left behind them the rocks which had been misty and*
> *soft hardened and were marked with red clefts.* (*W*, 21)

References to blue and green will recur throughout the text, the opening sections themselves echoing a short story by Katherine Mansfield, 'At the Bay' (1922). Conversation and setting have largely been eliminated in Woolf, however. *The Waves* is a novel about the things people do not say but feel and think. We know a great deal about the mental worlds of Rhoda, Jinny, Susan, Louis, Bernard and Neville, but not how they look or even speak; the prosaic has no place. Ironically, the work of Woolf's final ten years – *Flush*, *The Years*, *Three Guineas*, *Roger Fry* and *Between the Acts* – reverses this situation. It concentrates on realistic detail such as the domestic details of Wimpole Street in *Flush* or what Roger Fry read on the Orient Express when he returned to England from Turkey in 1911 surrounded by the pottery and scarfs he had purchased.[29] In these works, Woolf includes what *The Waves* excludes.

What the novel partly deals with is time, the synchronic trumping the diachronic; the reader is told at one point that Neville thinks 'with the unlimited time of the mind which stretches in a flash from Shakespeare to ourselves' (*w*, 228). Life does not unfold like an arrow but turns and twists and repeats, rearranging experience. Life is not orderly, nor methodical. Death unexpectedly interferes, as in the death of Percival in India from a fall off his horse. Yet, for a novel that intensifies solitude in both method and action, it is surprising to read that 'life withers when there are things we cannot share' (*w*, 221).

The novel, especially at the end with Bernard's long soliloquy, establishes 'disillusioned clarity' while admitting that if there are no stories 'what end can there be, or what beginning?' Perhaps life is not susceptible 'to the treatment we give it when we try to tell it' (*w*, 222, 223), although Woolf includes a wide-ranging list of writers from Shakespeare to Byron, Meredith and Dostoevsky. Their appearance, or at least reference to them, gives agency to literature and the power of stories seen in Woolf's earlier works.

One of the more important allusions in the novel is to Virgil, who appears repeatedly in Woolf, beginning with Chapter Twelve of *Jacob's Room*, where Erasmus Cowan sips port and recites Virgil and Catullus. Mr Carmichael reads Virgil's *Georgics* in *To the Lighthouse* and Chapter Three of *A Room of One's Own* refers to the ancient Roman poet. In *The Waves*, Virgil with Catullus become a preoccupation of Neville's thoughts. This should not be a surprise given Virgil's prominence among modern writers, cited for example by Freud, who has an epigraph by him on the title page of *The Interpretation of Dreams*.

Woolf had difficulty finding a form for her story, remarking in 1927 in a comment on Vita's *Passenger to Teheran* that 'the method of writing smooth narrative can't be right; things don't happen in one's mind like that' (*D*, III, 126–7). But three years later a diary entry for December 1930 records a moment of integration, of remaking the story, which occurred while listening to a Beethoven quartet. At that instant she thought that she might 'merge all the interjected passages into Bernard's final speech, & end with the words O solitude: thus making him absorb all those scenes & having no further break' (*D*, III, 339). This also shows that the theme of effort, of energetically pursuing a set of goals, dominates, not 'the waves: & personality: & defiance' (*D*, III, 339). In August 1930 Woolf wrote that the novel was resolving itself 'into a series of dramatic soliloquies' but the thing is to keep them 'running homogeneously in & out, in the rhythm of the waves' (*D*, III, 312). To Ethyl Smith, composer and musician, she explained in August 1930 that,

> I am writing to a rhythm and not to a plot . . . And thus
> though the rhythmical is more natural to me than the
> narrative, it is completely opposed to the tradition of
> fiction and I am casting about all the time for some
> rope to throw to the reader. (*LETT*, IV, 204)

In the text of the novel, Bernard corroborates this view, saying 'how I distrust neat designs of life that are drawn upon half-sheets of notepaper' (*W*, 199), having earlier written 'the rhythm is the main thing in writing' (*W*, 63). But Woolf was unsure of the artistic effect 'because the proportions may need the intervention of the waves finally so as to make a conclusion' (*D*, III, 339). In this work, 'the normal is abolished' (*W*, 97); only nature offers coherency, not society, history or individual action. The sequence of things is abolished in favour of the rhythm of nature and life, although we pretend life is 'a solid substance, shaped like a globe, which we turn about in our fingers' (*W*, 210).

Of the six characters, Bernard has the greatest need for the company of others. But like Rhoda and Louis, Neville is one of Bernard's defectors and remains an outsider. His idealistic perfectionism, rooted in the Classics, keeps him separate from the orbit of others, but like Rhoda he is deeply susceptible to beauty: 'that would be a glorious life, to addict oneself to perfection; to follow the curve of the sentence' (*W*, 70). He hopes to be a poet but his scholarly temperament prevents him from attaining the imaginative state necessary. Bernard, by contrast, is a phrasemaker and storyteller. He keeps a notebook where he records his observations and phrases. During his college years, he even self-consciously constructed an image of himself as a Byronic figure 'who, lightly throwing off his cloak, seizes his pen' (*W*, 62).

To 'set this hubbub in order' may be the ostensible goal of *The Waves*, but Woolf knew it was impossible (*W*, 149). Each sight is 'an arabesque scrawled suddenly to illustrate some hazard and marvel of intimacy' (*W*, 178). In the end is confusion: 'this is not one life; nor do I always know if I am man or woman, Bernard or Neville, Louis, Susan, Jinny or Rhoda – so strange is the contact of one with another', writes Bernard (*W*, 234). But that is the point: life is to be lived, not to be analysed or made to fit an imposed and artificial order, says Bernard. It is impossible 'to keep coherency'; 'The wave has tumbled me over', he laments with resignation at the end (*W*, 244).

With her success and status at this time, Woolf and Leonard began to travel again; one of their strangest voyages was a motor trip to

Europe in April 1935 that included Nazi Germany. This was a troubling journey, not least because the Nuremberg laws against Jews had recently been passed, presenting an obvious danger to Leonard (who distracted the border guards when entering the country with his marmoset Mitz). The increasing power of Hitler and persecution of the Jews did not seem to concern either Woolf or Leonard, who wanted to witness at first hand the changes taking place in Germany. Unknowingly, they drove through Bonn as it prepared for a citywide reception of Goering, the streets lined with anti-Jewish banners. Seeing Mitz, however, the crowds cheered, shouting 'Heil Hitler!' in appreciation of the odd English couple driving down the main street. Woolf raised her own arm in response.[30]

Angelica Garnett (neé Bell) and Virginia Woolf, 1932.

Why they went to Germany in the first place remains unclear, yet Woolf's actions address her contradictory views concerning Jews, despite her marriage to Leonard. A scene in *The Years* has Sara Pargiter in cheap lodgings disgusted at having to share a bath with a Jewish man, fearful he will dirty the tub. Woolf's short story of 1937, 'The Duchess and the Jeweller', is about a poverty-stricken Jewish male who becomes the richest jeweller in London; elements of anti-Semitism appear throughout and it was initially rejected by American magazines, although it finally appeared, after some changes, in *Harper's Bazaar*. Woolf did, however, occasionally acknowledge her complicity in anti-Semitism through partial self-accusation. In August 1930 she confessed to Ethel Smyth 'how I hated marrying a Jew – how I hated their nasal voices, and their oriental jewellery, and their noses and their wattles – what a snob I was: for they have immense vitality, and I think I like that quality best of all' (*LETT*, IV, 195–6).

Nevertheless, during this period of turmoil in Europe, Woolf's popularity rose. The sales of her books increased: in their first year of publication *Jacob's Room* sold 1,413 in the UK; *Mrs Dalloway* sold 2,236; *To the Lighthouse* was more successful, selling 3,873. *Orlando* was the turning point: it sold more in Britain in the first month than *To the Lighthouse* in a year, reaching a total of 21,135 in six months. There was a levelling out with *The Waves* but *Flush*, her biography of Elizabeth Barrett Browning's dog, rekindled interest. In six months, 18,739 copies were sold in Britain and 14,081 in the U.S. Her most commercially successful book was *The Years*, published in 1937, selling 43,909 in its first six months – 13,005 in Britain and 30,904 in the U.S. She was so popular that her picture – a photograph by Man Ray – appeared on the cover of *Time* magazine. In later years figures reversed, with *To the Lighthouse* outselling *Mrs Dalloway*, which outsold *Orlando*, *The Waves* and *The Years*.[31]

In volume II of *An Autobiography*, Leonard Woolf is especially keen to emphasize that while Woolf enjoyed a reputation as a serious novelist and was reviewed widely, she was not a popular writer. *Orlando, Flush* and *The Years* were 'immeasurably more successful' than any of her other books. *The Years* was indeed the most successful but, in Leonard's words, 'the worst book she ever wrote'.[32] *Orlando* and *Flush* are only *jeu d'esprit,* he adds. By 1928, when Woolf was 46, she had published five novels and despite enjoying a serious reputation, she could not live off her earnings. Queenie Leavis, wife of the Cambridge critic F. R. Leavis, called her novels 'highbrow art', echoing Arnold Bennett who called Woolf 'Queen of the High-brows' in an article in the *Evening Standard* on 28 November 1929.[33] For all the excellences of *To the Lighthouse*, it was not a popular book.[34] The readership of Woolf, though esteemed, was small.

7

Monk's House I, 1919–37

Monk's House, purchased for £700 by the Woolfs in 1919 and owned until 1969, was continually improved by the Woolfs as monies permitted. Located in pastoral East Sussex, with its open garden stretching to the South Downs at the rear of the house, and its front bordering a narrow street in the village of Rodmell, the home and surrounding landscape provided the necessary respite from personal distress and private loss. But operating it was a challenge: the kitchen was damp and dark; there was no electricity, gas, or running water. It lacked a bathroom, having only an earth privy in the garden. Water had to be pumped and carried in and the stove, installed only in 1920, had to be lit daily and kept going with fuel which had to be gathered before even preparing a cup of tea. Before the installation of the stove, the Woolfs relied on the oven of a Mrs Dedman, the wife of the village Sexton. Her husband, William, was the initial Monk's House gardener. Mrs Dedman regularly brought over stews and mashes. The Woolfs also had a 'daily', a village girl who came each day to clean, supplementing their reliable if tiresome cook/servant from London, Nellie Boxall.[1]

Water occasionally flooded the kitchen floor, with mud sometimes entering through the doorways. Even sound could not be contained: the uncovered oak floorboards amplified every step. Leonard and Woolf took baths in the kitchen behind a curtain. They first shared a large upstairs bedroom (each in their own single bed) but after a servant left, Leonard moved into one of two small rooms across the landing. Woolf, who disliked live-in servants, gradually tried to oversee the house with only one servant, although occasionally help would join them from the village, where they owned two small cottages. There was an informality in the household: no one dressed for dinner, Woolf often writing to friends not to bring clothes when coming to stay. Nonetheless, a bell was still rung at mealtimes, although no table linen was used.

But in 1919, the Woolfs also faced several financial challenges: Leonard's job with the *International Review* had ended, forcing them to consider reducing their household staff. When the lease ran out on Hogarth House, which included the adjoining Suffield House, they used a portion of their capital to buy both properties, letting out Suffield House for a year. They had already bought Monk's House. When they moved from Hogarth House to Tavistock Square in London in 1924, they let their old house for three years. They were landlords, the more so when they acquired two small cottages in Rodmell, one in 1928 for Leonard's gardener and a year later one for Annie Thompsett, a new servant who came in daily but, to the delight of the Woolfs, left by three o'clock so that they were alone for the remainder of the day, something of an innovation in British domestic practice.

One other feature of Monk's House stood out: the garden, which was Leonard's preserve. He grew vegetables, enriched by substantial greenhouses and plants that reminded him of Ceylon. He also spent money on a new oak gate and new millstones for a path to the front of the house. In 1928 the Woolfs bought an adjacent field, adding an acre to the garden, and put up a fence to keep local children out. Woolf remarked uneasily that that was 'my first act as a landowner'. At its most extensive, the entire area of Monk's House and grounds measured 6.5 acres (D, III: 193–4, 184, n.4)

In 1931 the Woolfs added a garage, acknowledging their mutual interest in automobiles, which offered them mobility, travel and adventure. Earlier, in 1924, however, Woolf published a column critical of the automobile. Entitled 'The Cheapening of Motor-cars', it critiqued how cars were ruining the countryside as macadam replaced gravel and the vehicles replaced foot and horse traffic. Cyclists in particular found themselves in danger. In the essay, Woolf opposes the increasing domination of the car, although by the summer of 1927, she and Leonard were part of this new movement, purchasing the first of two Singers, which were relatively inexpensive vehicles.

Woolf was almost giddy with anticipation in July 1927, just days before the first Singer arrived – the purchase made possible, as discussed in Chapter Six, because of advance sales of *To the Lighthouse*: 'This is a great opening up in our lives. One may go to Bodiam, to Arundel, explore the Chichester downs, expand that curious thing, the map of the world in ones [*sic*] mind.' 'It will I think demolish loneliness', she adds (D, III, 147). Ironically, neither Leonard nor Woolf could drive, although they immediately began lessons. Their second Singer, purchased in February 1929, was an early form of convertible with a chain-driven sliding roof. Their library by now included George Morland's *Motoring without Trouble*, *The Owner-driver's ABC* and John Prioleau's *Car & Country: Week-end Signposts to the Open Road*. Woolf shared her excitement with both Vita Sackville-West and T. S. Eliot, who were also car enthusiasts.

The first Singer was likely a Singer 14/34, followed by a Singer Sunshine Saloon in 1929. By 1932 the Woolfs moved up to a Lanchester 18, a luxury car costing at least twice as much as either Singer. They purchased the silver and green six-cylinder Lanchester, with its advanced 'fluid fly wheel' transmission, in late 1932 (delivered in January 1933), after attending the 1932 Olympia Motor Show in London. Horsepower topped out at 58 bhp at 3,800 rpm with a tested maximum speed of 71 mph (114 km/h). Woolf's diary records her pride and excitement with the car, which offered an implied cultural status, echoing the car that Clarissa Dalloway hears and sees when she is buying flowers on Bond Street. That car, with its mysterious passenger, seemed headed to Buckingham Palace, but a punctured tyre forced it to the side of the road. Woolf actually did not own a car when she wrote *Mrs Dalloway*, but by the time of the Lanchester, she could write that, while driving it, 'I feel ever so rich, conservative, patriotic, religious and humbuggish . . . and I enjoy this new Virginia immensely' (*LETT*, 5, 154). The car came with a fold-out windshield and sunroof.

Monk's House became a refuge for the pair, increasingly so as the years passed. As death began to surround them, escape to the tranquillity and isolation of Monk's House became essential. But there was also much socializing at Charleston, where Vanessa lived with Clive Bell and Duncan Grant nearby, as well as Tilton, the farmhouse close to Charleston where the Keyneses lived. Parties were frequently held at all three locations, with the servants also normally invited, and often there were high spirits. Woolf reported in her diary of an August 1928 visit from E. M. Forster: he was 'timid, touchy and infinitely charming'. Nevertheless, they both got drunk and 'talked of sodomy, & sapphism, with emotion' (*D*, III, 193).

In the period following the publication of *The Waves*, the death of more close friends occurred, beginning with Lytton Strachey in 1932 and the suicide of his long-term partner Dora Carrington the day after Woolf visited her. Woolf felt the loss of Strachey acutely, and the day he died, although she had not yet had the news, she wrote 'it is like having the globe of the future perpetually smashed – without Lytton' (*D*, IV, 64). Two years after Strachey's death, Roger Fry died, the same year as George Duckworth. These losses – and others such as D. H. Lawrence in 1930, Arnold Bennett in 1931, G. L. Dickinson in 1932 and John Galsworthy in 1933 marking the decline if not disappearance of the Bloomsbury generation – partly explain Woolf's increasing turn to the autobiographical essay.

Woolf's interest in autobiographical writing began as early as 1906 with her essay 'Impressions of Sir Leslie Stephen'. In that early work, Virginia Stephen creates herself as the literary descendent of her father by describing his reading habits. In her 1932 appreciation

Lytton Strachey and Virginia Woolf with Lord David Cecil, June 1923, photograph by Lady Ottoline Morrell.

of him, simply titled 'Leslie Stephen', she fashions herself as his child but says little about her contradictory relationship with him which mixed criticism with adoration.[2] Most importantly, all of her autobiographical writings remained unpublished during her lifetime as they were written either to be spoken or circulated privately.[3] However, during this period she also began to write a family saga – *The Years* – perhaps an elegy to her own notion of family.

Originally called *The Pargiters*, Woolf began work on the text in October 1932 and it quickly became a work that plagued her until it appeared in March 1937. Its form and treatment of history were the biggest challenges, the work originating in a diary note made the day before she was to give a speech to the London and National Society for Women's Service in January 1931. In the note she suddenly conceived of a sequel to *A Room of One's Own*; the book would be about the sexual lives of women. It was to be called 'Professions for Women' (*D*, IV, 6), and in her diary she wrote a possible title: *Here & Now*. In her diary of December 1932, she added that the new work, titled then 'The Pargiters', was 'first cousin to Orlando, though the cousin in the flesh' (*D*, IV, 133). Thinking of the new work, she wrote, 'releases such a torrent of fact as I did not know I had in me . . . of course this is external: but there's a good deal of gold – more than I'd thought – in externality' (*D*, IV, 133). She hoped to marry this to a 'Poet's book', a work of vision to match the world of fact. At the same time, Vita completed a novel entitled *Family History*, published by the Hogarth Press in October 1932 and possibly a spur to Woolf's own intentions in *The Years*.

Woolf's goal was as ambitious as it was unattainable. The book, she wrote,

> should include satire, comedy, poetry, narrative, & what form is to hold them all together? Should I bring in a play, letters, poems? I think I begin to grasp the whole. And it's to end with the press of daily normal life continuing. And there are to be millions of ideas but no preaching – history, politics, feminism, art, literature – in short a summing up of all I know, feel, laugh at, despise, like, admire, hate & so on. (*D*, IV, 152)

In the end, Woolf realized it would have to be two separate books: a novel and a political work, which became first *The Years* and then a polemical censure of militarist patriarchy, *Three Guineas.* For the next eighteen months or so, Woolf read extensively in preparation for what would become the book on women and family life (*The Years*) and then her critique of patriarchy (*Three Guineas*). Later, she would say the two works constituted one book. An original draft, entitled 'The Pargiters, A Novel-Essay', unsuccessfully tried to alternate fictional extracts from a novel with essays of factual commentary. During this period she was also working on *Flush*, the biography of Elizabeth Barrett Browning's dog, a kind of relief or at least alternative from the lengthy family saga she was constructing – *The Years* became her second longest novel after *Night and Day*.

In January 1933 Woolf visualized the book as having a 'curiously uneven time sequence – a series of great balloons, linked by straight narrow passages of narrative' (*D*, IV, 142). By February that year she expanded this vision, seeking to incorporate sections of commentary directly into the text in a more ambitious work. In her diary she wrote,

> I want to give the whole of the present society – nothing less: facts, as well as vision. And to combine them both. I mean, The Waves going on simultaneously with Night & Day . . . It should aim at immense breadth and immense intensity. (*D*, IV, 151–2)

Woolf would ultimately cut the social commentary – saving it for *Three Guineas* – and trim the narrative authority of several of the novel's more political characters, notably Sarah, an anti-war feminist, and Nicholas, a homosexual utopianist. In February 1933 she wrote that she would leave out the inter-chapters; they would

Virginia Woolf at Monk's House, 1935.

probably be too propagandistic. Throughout the novel she stresses characters in conflict with institutions: the government, the military, the law, universities or the family. She also saturates the novel with objects; when the street lamp illuminates a room in the '1907' section, it spotlights 'a tray of glasses on the hall table; a top-hat; and a chair with gilt paws. The chair . . . had a look of ceremony; as if it stood on the cracked floor of some Italian ante-room.' (*Y*, 126)

In March 1936, a further diary entry outlined the continuous personal and historical threats that were taking place as she worked:

> This is the most feverish overworked political week we've
> yet had. Hitler has his army on the Rhine. Meetings taking
> place in London . . . as usual, I think Oh this will blow over.
> But its [*sic*] odd, how near the guns have got to our private
> life again. I can quite distinctly see them & hear a roar, even
> though I go on like a doomed mouse, nibbling at my daily page.
> (*D*, V, 17)

That spring she also suffered from depression and illness, writing in her diary that she had 'never been so near the precipice to my own feeling since 1913' (*D*, V, 24).

The conflict between the private self and the outside world creates a tension that Woolf confronted throughout all of her writing in the 1930s. The Hogarth Press responded to the conflict of the times by publishing a series of public pieces, *The Hogarth Letters* (1933), written in reaction to the collapse of the Labour government in 1931, the rise of Nazism and anti-Semitism and the coming threat of war. Woolf's 'Letter to a Young Poet' appeared in the series, containing an implicit debate between art and propaganda which her 1940 essay 'The Leaning Tower' restated. Her essay 'Why Art Today Follows Politics', published in *The Daily Worker* in December 1936, laments the inescapability of the artist from politics. Yet she also questioned the value of action for the artist: 'I think action generally unreal. It's the thing we do in the dark that is more real', she wrote to Stephen Spender (*LETT*, VI, 122).

The text of *The Years*, the last of her novels to appear in print during her lifetime, literally annotates its own title. Chapter One is 1880, followed by 1891, then 1907, 1908, 1910, 1911, 1914 and so on until the longest section, simply titled 'The Present Day', forming eleven chapters in total. Each section, beginning with a panoramic overview of political, social and even natural conditions before focusing on the consciousness of individual characters, covers a single day, with the exception of the first, which deals with at least three days. The novel covers fifty years and became her best-selling work, even appearing in an American Armed Forces edition for distribution to soldiers during the Second World War.

The story essentially chronicles the lives of the Pargiters, the novel a summing up of Woolf's contemporary interests, from family to university education, politics (especially the suffragettes), India, music, marriage, war and people. A party held by Delia Pargiter in the final section ends the novel like *Mrs Dalloway*. It is a scene of family members confronting each other with varying degrees of acceptance. North Pargiter finds tolerance of his sister Peggy in a line from Catullus, which softens his frustration with her constant criticism of him and his attempts at writing (*Y*, 374). North, frustrated with London after years of farming in Africa, believes all people talk about in London is money and politics (*Y*, 380). The novel ends with the arrival of dawn as the party breaks up, with the sun rising above the house wearing 'an air of extraordinary beauty, simplicity and peace', a somewhat ironic set piece given Woolf's struggle to complete the novel, although it may also reflect her relief at finally finishing the work, which she felt strongly to have been a failure (*Y*, 413).

Nevertheless, *The Years* provides a dialogue-filled social and political panorama of England between 1890 and 1937, but one that prefers to whitewash history. The word 'parget', in fact, means to plaster over or to whitewash and is the likely origin of the family name. The book is saved though from the confinements of realist fiction found in the works of writers like Bennett, Galsworthy or Wells, by Woolf's effort to combine fact and vision, which she highlighted in a 1933 essay on Turgenev where she remarked that he 'has to observe facts impartially, yet he must also interpret them . . . but few combine the fact and the vision', although he apparently succeeds.[4]

Accessible, detailed, historic, descriptive, *The Years* was a bestseller in both Britain and America. It was structurally undemanding from a reader's point of view, although personally challenging and difficult for Woolf to write. Its publication was an event, especially in America, and led to her photo by Man Ray appearing on the cover of *Time* magazine in April 1937. *The Years* quickly reached the best-seller list and was the sixth most popular book of the year according to *Publishers Weekly*'s best-seller list for 1937 – a year of outstanding literary achievement. First on the list was *Gone with the Wind* by Margaret Mitchell; eighth was *Of Mice and Men* by John Steinbeck.

The events of history referred to in *The Years* range from the general election of 1880 to the deaths of Parnell and Edward vii, the air raids on London in the First World War and the establishment of the Irish Free State. They provided readers, especially in America, with a vivid sense of the major events in recent British history, while references to India and Africa exposed elements of the transnational. The seemingly fractured narrative sections mirrored the ruptured times. Lacking the experimentation of her other works, *The Years* possessed, in Woolf's words, 'more "real" life in it; more blood & bone' than her other works (*D*, v, 38). As the *New York Times* reviewer claimed, it was a relief from the discontinuity of *Jacob's Room* and the avant-garde structure of *The Waves*. *The Years* offered solidity of place and character, while the family, through fifty years of loss, setbacks, small triumphs and doubts, still lived with expectations. It is 'rich and lovely with the poetry of life', the reviewer writes, more like a poem or piece of music, and with 'a perfect beginning and a perfect end, and almost no middle'.[5]

8

Monk's House II, 1938–41

By the late 1930s Monk's House was no longer a quiet refuge but a centre of discontent. Where she once wrote in her diary of a May tree 'like a breaking wave outside; and all the garden green tunnels, mounds of green' (*D*, IV, 109), new physical if not mental boundaries appeared, whether orchard walls or Woolf's periods of unhappiness and mental collapse. As she confided earlier in her diary of 1921, 'Here [at Monk's House] I am chained to my rock: forced to do nothing; doomed to let every worry, spite, irritation & obsession scratch & claw & come again' (*D*, II, 132). The depression, despair and death described in this passage returned with a vengeance in Woolf's later years as she struggled against a growing mental and political darkness, despite the efforts of Leonard to stabilize her life.

Woolf again faced a period of accumulating and accelerating deaths, rather than new friendships. Woolf's nephew Julian Bell died in 1937 while fighting in the Spanish Civil War. Lady Ottoline Morrell died in April 1938; Yeats, Freud and Ford Madox Ford in 1939. Two months before her own suicide in March 1941, Woolf learned that James Joyce had died (*D*, V, 352). Close personal friends, as well as the avant-garde champions of 1920s modernism, were disappearing. The impending Second World War further aggravated her state of mind, despite a final summer party at Charleston in August 1939.

A previous moment of fun was the production in 1923 of Woolf's play *Freshwater* about her great-aunt, the photographer Julia Margaret Cameron. As early as 30 January 1919 she thought of a play about Julia's life, beginning with Charles Hay Cameron, who for twelve years did not go beyond his garden and then suddenly walked down to the sea. He and his wife, the photographer, then decide to voyage to Ceylon (in the play, India) 'taking their coffins with them'. Her last sight of her Aunt Julia is on board ship presenting to the porters large photographs of Sir Henry Taylor and the Madonna 'in default of small change' (*D*, I, 237).

Performed in Vanessa's studio at 8 Fitzroy Street in January 1935, a week before Woolf's 53rd birthday, the re-written *Freshwater* permitted (in the style of *Orlando*) family jokes, gags about bisexuality and even an appearance by Tennyson. Vanessa played Julia Cameron, Leonard was her husband Charles and Woolf's sixteen-year-old niece Angelica was Ellen Terry. Julian was the handsome naval officer John Craig, who runs off with Ellen (Angelica). The audience of eighty included Elizabeth Bowen, David Cecil, David Garnett and Clive Bell.

But Woolf was not above getting into conflicts at this time, beginning with Leonard, whom she had begun to find rigid and methodical. He in turn was cross with her because she was still smoking, despite efforts to cut down. He was also irritated by her preference for making holiday arrangements in favour of her family and not the two of them. The London Library also upset her when they refused to change their policy of no memberships for women, a tradition which had been supported by her father, Sir Leslie Stephen, and had been another point of conflict between the two. Female exclusion again stared her in the face and she was angered.

Also worrying her was the thought that her work would be forgotten or consigned to literary history. Wyndham Lewis noted in *Men without Art* (1934) that no one took Woolf seriously any more. The first book-length study of Woolf, appearing in 1932 by Winifred Holtby, concluded that Woolf's range would 'remain limited, her contact with life delicate', and she would not command a large public audience.[1] The backlash against modernism soon took the

form of canonization and fossilization. As early as 1931 Harold
Nicolson celebrated Woolf, Joyce, Eliot, Lawrence and Waugh as
'modern' writers of the post-war period in a BBC radio broadcast;
Woolf was offended because the statement implied that she was
'done'.[2] Even *Flush* met with resistance, critics suggesting that Woolf
was growing less interested in using her technique as a method to
explore reality, than using this method to try and create her own
reality. The resulting anxiety over her status informed her late work,
extending her early sensitivity to the judgement of others of her
writing. Turning to social and political commentary in her last
decade was one way of reacting against such criticism. Her challenge
to the values of masculine high literary culture, underscored by
political instability, was another.

From the outset, *Three Guineas* was controversial. Q. D. Leavis,
again critical of Woolf, was openly opposed to it; in a review in 1938
she declared that the book was not 'really reviewable' because it was
merely a conversation between Woolf and her social class, limiting
men to functioning only 'at Westminster', while women do no
more than shop. Mrs Woolf, Leavis claimed, was not living in the
contemporary world. In fact, her class only succeeded in insulating
her, although Woolf had benefited from that isolation. To complain
of the rights of women was almost ludicrous given Woolf's
advantages. Furthermore, she wrote, 'This book is not merely silly
and ill-informed, though it is that too, it contains some dangerous
assumptions, some preposterous claims and some nasty attitudes.'[3]
Using 'feminine inconsequence' as a weapon was hardly an
argument; the impact, Leavis caustically writes, was 'like Nazi
dialectic without Nazi conviction'. Woolf, it seems, wanted the
women of her class 'to have the privileges of womanhood without
the duties and responsibilities'.[4] Leavis adds that the photographs
in the book of men dressed for power had been 'selected with
malice'; a set of women equally dressed could easily have been
compiled. The photographs defeated themselves.[5]

Vita was similarly upset, telling Woolf that her book advanced 'misleading arguments' that approached dishonesty.[6] Woolf responded angrily, asking Vita to explain; did she mean that she marshalled the facts in a dishonest manner to produce a certain effect? It was beyond anything an honest book, Woolf claimed, telling Vita that she took 'more pains to get up the facts and state them plainly than I ever took with anything in my life'. But the animosity remained, Woolf telling Vita that she could not bring herself to read Vita's latest poem 'Solitude' impartially 'while your charges against me . . . remain unsubstantiated'. Numerous exchanges followed until Woolf felt that she was not accused of dishonesty.[7]

The telling photographs in *Three Guineas* – photographs Leavis does *not* mention – are the ones that are, in fact, *not* there: those of the unidentified civilians killed in the Spanish Civil War, described but not reproduced in the text.[8] They function to register trauma, echoing Freud, who applied the metaphor of the camera to explain the unconscious as the place where traumatic memory-bits remain captured until resolved.[9] Rather than being understood as having captured past time, photographs of traumatic events access time and events that are distinct and explosive but not yet integrated into consciousness. They register in the psyche, as do the photographs of the dead for Woolf. The photograph is not a narrative but the embodiment of trauma itself, time as a single devastating burst of experience. The photographs' capturing of 'unexperienced events' parallels the structure of traumatic memory.[10] The grip of the event on memory and the imagination is precisely because it was not experienced but witnessed later in a photograph. In these instances, seeing is a form of not knowing.

Emily Dalgarno, in *Virginia Woolf and the Visible World* (2001) points out how Woolf relied on the visual textuality of the Spanish photographs to question the historical connection between patriarchal society and war. Penalties made visible are what Woolf seeks to

Virginia Woolf in the garden at Garsington, June 1926, photo by Lady
Ottoline Morrell.

undermine, doing so through association: 'Can we bring out the
connection between them [war photos] and prostituted culture and
intellectual slavery' to make it 'clear that the one implies the other',
she asks.[11] While her preparatory notebooks for *Three Guineas*
document abuses of British patriarchy, the photos broaden her
vision, situating her question – how to prevent war? – in the context
of European culture.

The use of the letter form in *Three Guineas* underscores a sense
of the book constituting a continued dialogue with Woolf's dead

Virginia Woolf's desk in the writing lodge in the garden of Monk's House.

nephew Julian Bell, while the deployment of the photographs confronts the artistic and moral problems generated by the use of such tragic images for propaganda purposes. But avoiding the sensationalism of images that appeared in, say, *The Daily Worker*, are the substituted images of male power, which at the same time suggest a connection between violence and male authority. Not publishing the Spanish Civil War pictures allows Woolf to turn the images into a universal illustration of the evils of war, which gain even greater currency because they are fictionalized (that is, exist only in generalized descriptive language). There is no rendering of wounds or mutilation; as a consequence, they become metaphors of a stylized war.

Images are the vehicle of collective memory. They are the preferred way to maintain past knowledge, something Woolf instinctively understood from her earliest published writing on photography, comments on Julia Margaret Cameron in the 1926 Hogarth Press volume *Victorian Photographs of Famous Men and*

Fair Women. Woolf invested in photographic imagery and commentary from an early age. Her diaries, letters and essays address photographic matters and she uses photographic terms descriptively in her fiction. Before and during her marriage to Leonard, she took, developed and preserved photographs in a series of albums. More than twenty references to photography appear in the first year, 1897, of Woolf's first published journal. By 1904, when she and her siblings first moved to Bloomsbury, photography was a constant presence in her life.[12] The following year she implored Violet Dickinson to buy photographs during her American tour. And despite new pocket Kodak models appearing yearly from 1895 onwards, many of which she acquired, Woolf was thrilled with Leonard's purchase of a more expensive Zeiss camera bought in 1931 with 'violent impetuosity', as she told Ethel Smyth.

Woolf frequently exchanged photographs with friends and family, who were all energetic, if amateur, photographers. Lady Ottoline Morrell, Vita Sackville-West and Dora Carrington all traded photos with Woolf. She sent not one but two photographs to Leonard before their marriage in case he did not like her first choice, which she thought too noble. When married, she and Leonard both took photography seriously, his diaries regularly recording expenditures for photographic supplies. Leonard took photos not only of Virginia but of Virginia and Vita together.[13]

She constantly asked friends to send her photos, and those of now-deceased friends were especially important; for example, she requested a snapshot from the widow of the French painter Jacques Raverat, who died in 1924. Woolf even used photographs to lure Vita Sackville-West. Writing to her in 1924, she asked Vita to visit to look at her great-aunt's photos of Tennyson and others. In late 1927 Woolf arranged for photographs of Vita to be taken for *Orlando*. She also used photos to help her write. In 1931 Woolf asked Vita for one of Harold Nicolson's cocker spaniel Henry, which became the physical basis of Flush, the dog of Elizabeth Barrett Browning in

Woolf's work of the same name. Woolf's collection of photograph albums, the Monk's House Albums, reflect a similar investment in photographic records.

Woolf also used photographic terms in descriptive passages in her fiction. Her use of photographs in *Flush*, *Three Guineas* and *Orlando* parallel the many references to photography in her novels, as in *Jacob's Room*, *Night and Day* and even in the tonal quality of *To the Lighthouse*, reflecting the imagery of Julia Margaret Cameron. Her short story 'Portraits' uses specific photographic vocabulary, while her photo scrapbooks actually became resources for the imagery in *Three Guineas*. Earlier in Woolf's work, in the novel *Night and Day*, the photographs that people display in their homes outline their character. At the end of *The Years*, when Eleanor sees the photograph in her paper of an unnamed tyrant, likely Mussolini, she angrily tears it up.

Despite her interest in photography, Woolf disliked to be professionally photographed, although she appeared in *Vogue*, *Harper's Bazaar*, *Time* and the national press. She also objected to 'paparazzi': the relentless photographing of private people, writers, artists and their homes, as well as their gardens, studios, bedrooms and writing tables (*LETT*, V, 238). The invasion of privacy was to her untenable. She refused to be photographed by Cecil Beaton and was furious at appearing in a collection of his images, writing that she was never asked, never sat and 'never saw the horrid worm' but 'there I am seized forever' (*LETT*, IV, 258). Sitting in 1939 for Gisèle Freund, who had photographed James Joyce, Walter Benjamin and Sylvia Beach, seemed to Woolf like 'being hoisted about on top of a stick for anyone to stare at' (*LETT*, VI, 351).

The visual impact of unavoidable trauma is evident throughout *Three Guineas*, even though its presentation is visually circumscribed. The generalized but repeated presence of the photographs of the maimed and destroyed in Spain allows Woolf to both engage and disengage from its horror, which she understands is a persistant experience of wartime. The trauma of death and destruction does not disappear, reflecting of course her ongoing encounter with trauma in her personal life. The photographs repeat and remind her of moments of crisis and loss that she has directly experienced, sustaining the often repressed trauma narrative of her life, ironized in the book by the regal, authoritative images of British men of power. The trauma of Spain, underscored by the death of her nephew, anticipates the trauma of the Second World War and the possible destruction of Britain, which accelerated her own sense of despair and ultimately led to her suicide. The medium of Woolf's recovery from trauma, however, was writing: 'It is only by putting [trauma] into words that I make it whole', she wrote in 'A Sketch of the Past'. 'A shock is at once in my case followed by the desire to explain it.'[14] This process reintegrates the trauma into an individual's life story.

In *Three Guineas* photographs function as fact, even though Woolf is aware of the way they misrepresent and limit one's vision of an event. Throughout the work, she criticizes photography with confidence, concluding *Three Guineas* by offering a further critique of a photograph (of a man in uniform). She also addresses private and public fear, and exhibits a clarity at the end that displays a new-found certainty obtained through her analysis and use of photographs. Confronting her interlocutor, she writes that 'as we listen to the voices of the past' it seems 'as if we were looking at the photographs again, at the picture of dead bodies and ruined houses that the Spanish Government sends us almost weekly', but with new understanding. And she emphasizes that history repeats itself: 'pictures and voices are the same today as they were 2,000 years ago.' Woolf acknowledges that photography redeems as much as it disrupts.[15]

Ethel Smyth said of *Three Guineas*: 'your book is so splendid it makes me hot.'[16] Smyth offered the reaction of many. Woolf herself was thrilled to finish the proofs of the book – it freed her, because having committed herself, she was 'afraid of nothing. Can do anything I like. No longer famous, no longer on a pedestal . . . on my own forever. That's my feeling: a sense of expansion like putting on slippers.' She felt, though, that it was not a good book and 'will excite nothing but mild sneers' (*D*, v, 136–7).

Between *Three Guineas* and *Roger Fry*, Woolf read Freud, starting with *Moses and Monotheism* in March 1939, which the Hogarth Press published; indeed, they had been publishing translations of all of Freud's works, overseen by James Strachey, Lytton's brother, since 1924. On 28 January 1939 Woolf and Leonard visited Freud at 20 Maresfield Gardens in Hampstead. They met in his consulting room and although Woolf was seated on a chair, not his couch, she still felt like a patient. Conversation at the meeting, she reported, touched on Hitler and the war. In his memoirs Leonard provides an extended description of the Freud visit. In December 1939 Woolf turned to Freud's writings again 'to give my brain a wider scope'.[17]

In May 1939, because of noise and upheaval caused by demolition work in progress next door to them at Tavistock Square, the Woolfs moved again, a short distance away, to 37 Mecklenburgh Square just to the east of Coram's Fields. They spent much of their time, however, at Monk's House. A letter to Vita from 29 August 1939 shows Woolf's state of mind:

> I don't think I'm philosophic – rather numbed . . . L. gardening,
> playing bowls, cooking our dinner: and outside such a waste
> of gloom. Of course I'm not in the least patriotic, which may be
> a help, and not afraid, I mean for my own body. But that's an
> old body. And all the same I should like another ten years.[18]

During this troubling period Woolf turned her writing to non-fiction, working on her biography of Roger Fry, which was a difficult, frustrating book, as much for its reliance on facts that impeded the truth as for the impossibility of narrating the life of someone she knew so well. *Roger Fry: A Biography* was a book Woolf did not want to write, but she felt it was her duty, later referring to it as 'an experiment in self-suppression' (*LETT*, VI, 456). The text was laboured and fact-driven, as she herself realized (*LETT*, VI, 456). After attending Fry's funeral, which featured musical rather than spoken eulogies, Woolf noted that 'I like the wordlessness', but she also felt suddenly and powerfully a fear of her own death (*D*, IV, 243). Again, she lacked confidence: *The Years* had been an emotional drain and the hostility raised by some critics regarding *Three Guineas*, circulating in manuscript form, caused doubts. When she began her account of Fry in April 1938 – at the same time as she began *Pointz Hall*, to be retitled *Between the Acts* – she did so with a spirit of obligation. The Fry biography became more dutiful than she had imagined, partly because it was so personal for her. The more she grappled with it, the greater her doubt that she could write it. From the start she believed it would not be a good book, confirmed by Leonard's comment that it was inadequate. The book lacked the imaginative power of *Orlando* or even *Flush*.

One of the critical features of the biography was its focus on friendship. For Fry, 'if names mattered less and less, people mattered more and more.' 'How much they mattered', she continues in a comment on the limitations of biography, 'how from one end of his life to the other he lived in his friendships, how in letter after letter he broke into praise of his friends – all that is not to be conveyed by lists of names.'[19] Her reticence concerning Fry's friendships, however, originated not so much in Woolf's sense of protecting him, as her own anxiety about making the story too personal or intimate.

Ironically, shortly after *Roger Fry* was published on 25 July 1940, the threat of a German invasion of southern England almost reached a crescendo, Vita telling Woolf on 1 August 1940 that with things so uncertain, she would not think of suggesting a night to visit. Worry of the invasion had in fact reached such a level that Dr Adrian Stephen gave Woolf and Leonard lethal doses of morphine to be used in the event of an assault. Woolf, replying to Vita on 6 August

1940 about a possible meeting, writes that 'Great lorries are carrying sandbags down to the river: guns are being emplaced on the Banks. So do come before it's all ablaze.' On 9 August Vita reported that she had already moved her jewels and will to a safer place – the home of Harold Nicholson's brother, Eric, near Dartmoor – and that the only other treasure she had moved was the manuscript of *Orlando*.[20]

A diary entry from 29 September 1940 emphasizes the fear Woolf and Leonard experienced:

> They [the bombers] came very close. We lay down under the tree. The sound was like someone sawing in the air just above us. We lay flat on our faces. Hands behind head. Don't close y[ou]r teeth said L . . . bombs shook the window of my lodge. Will it drop I asked. If so, we shall be broken together. I thought, I think of nothingness – flatness, my mood being flat. Some fear I suppose. (*D*, v, 16)

Written with full awareness of the impending war and potential disaster for England and for herself and Leonard – by June 1940 the Nazis had stormed into France – Woolf turned to her novel *Between the Acts*, which reaches through the historical past to glimpse at an uncertain and clouded future. These events, plus the actual attacks on the country which were becoming more relentless, gave a melancholy if not desperate tone to her life and art during these years. The war, she noted in her diary, had 'taken away the outer wall of security. No echo comes back. I have no surroundings . . . We pour to the edge of a precipice . . . and then? I can't conceive that there will be a 27th June 1941.' On that same day, she tried 'to centre by reading Freud' (*D*, v, 299).

Fearful of an imminent end if the Germans invaded, Leonard, who had acquired extra petrol, thought they would end their lives inhaling carbon monoxide in their garage. But Woolf believed she should finish *Between the Acts*: 'oughtn't I to finish something by way of an end? The end gives its vividness, even its gaiety & recklessness to the random daily life' (*D*, v, 298). In preparation for writing her novel, Woolf read Elizabethan drama and, towards the book's completion, on 1 February 1941, during the Blitz, she wrote to Ethel Smyth about her review: 'Did I tell you I'm reading the whole of English literature through?' it begins:

> By the time I've reached Shakespeare the bombs will be falling. So I've arranged a very nice last scene: reading Shakespeare, having forgotten my gas mask. I shall fade far away, & quite forget . . . (*LETT*, VI, 466)

In *Between the Acts* Woolf abandoned the idea of a conventional narrative; rather, we get fragmentary glimpses into the minds of characters. An aloof narrator holds it all together. One point of view quickly replaces another, developing the technique of both *Jacob's Room* and *The Waves*. There are also no formal divisions between the different parts of the story, with no chapters or proper breaks. Narration almost silently slips between the subjective view of characters and back again to the objective view of a narrator. Echoes and repetitions work to unite the text. The overall irony of the work is that the historic elements of the pageant are contrasted with the small-scale individual dramas going on among the audience.

War framed most of Woolf's adult life: she was 32 when the First World War began and 59 when she ended her life in March 1941 after London was again bombed. The Old Bailey, the Guildhall and eight churches by Christopher Wren were badly damaged or destroyed in the raids of January 1941. In her diary for 6 August 1940 she notes: 'men excavating gun emplacements in the bank. They look like little swarms of busy ants, as I walk' (*D*, V, 310). On 19 August 1940 Woolf records that yesterday 'there was a roar. Right on top of us they came. I looked at the plane, like a minnow at a roaring shark . . . said to be 5 bombers hedge hopping on their way to London. The closest shave so far' (*D*, v, 312). Earlier, on 14 June 1940 – the day the Germans entered Paris – Vita, Leonard and Virginia had visited Penshurst Place in Kent. It was her first visit, although she had long been interested in it because it had been the home of Sir Philip Sidney, and she had written a long essay on his *Arcadia*.

A diary entry from 31 August 1940 begins with Woolf's recognition that England was finally being attacked. A phone call from Vita had troubled her because Vita held the receiver up so that Woolf could hear the exploding bombs. Almost comically, Woolf then went off and 'played bowls', but later that night there were 'planes zooming' and 'Explosions' in her own neighbourhood (*D*, v, 314). Her fear of an invasion intensified: 'Am I afraid? Intermittently. The worst of it is one's mind won't work with a spring next morning . . . this may be the beginning of invasion . . . I shall swim into quiet water', she adds prophetically (*D*, v, 314).

Woolf initially thought of *Between the Acts* as an antidote to the darkening political situation of the 1930s. In April 1938, she sought 'a rambling capricious but somehow unified whole' in the work (*D*, v, 135). She also hoped for a work that would relieve her mind of Roger Fry and asks for no scheme or 'cosmic immensities'. She sought something to 'amuse' herself (*D*, v, 135). A late letter from Woolf to Vita contextualizes *Between the Acts*, set in a 24-hour period in June 1939 and published posthumously. On 30 August 1940, Woolf writes that 'it's perfectly peaceful here – they're playing bowls – I'd just put flowers in your room. And there you sit with the bombs falling round you.'[21] The war, subtly and indeterminately, shadows the action in *Between the Acts*, from conversations to bombers heard overhead, all while Miss La Trobe attempts to recreate the grandeur of England in her historical pageant. Nonetheless, Woolf began the book as a playful diversion from her anti-war polemic *Three Guineas*. But the disruption of the Blitz poses not only physical but psychological danger, as Miss La Trobe's audience loses interest in the pageant. Even the moralizing reverend, pontificating about the pageant's theme, finds himself unsettled:

> Mr Streatfield paused. He listened. Did he hear some distant music? . . . the word was cut in two. A zoom severed it. Twelve aeroplanes in perfect formation like a flight of wild duck came overhead. That was the music, the audience gaped; the audience gazed. Then zoom became drone. The planes had passed.
>
> (*BA*, 173–4)

In this novel of interruptions, all becomes fractured, including the idea of a hero – for there is no hero. Giles Oliver is the only one with a stunted vision of the impending war; Lucy Swithin, elderly and Dallowayesque, is ineffectual; Miss La Trobe is stopped by her own anger and unhappiness; Isa Oliver, poet and mother, is too withdrawn to be effective. Identity itself resides in the 'in between', each figure possessing multiple nicknames. Incoherence, division, and soon war, looms for all. Language also reflects this unravelling: 'words cease to lie flat in the sentence', Woolf writes (*BA*, 55).

The mirrors reflecting the audience at the end of the pageant display a multiple and distorted self-constructed view of the people and their differences – and echo Mrs Oliver's 'three folded mirror' in which she can see three separate versions of herself (*BA*, 165, 12). Anticipating this is the pageant itself, which divides into three parts: after a prologue, the first scene is Shakespearean with romantic dialogue. The second parodies Restoration comedy and the third is a Victorian panorama based on a policeman directing traffic in Hyde Park. The final scene, 'Ourselves', surprises the audience when mirrors appear and turn upon the assembled.

Between the Acts, Woolf's last novel, like her first, focuses on place, this time an English country house, not London or South America as in *The Voyage Out*. Like her first novel, literature is again prominent, and Keats's 'Ode on a Grecian Urn' is referenced at the beginning and end of the novel. Correlating Isabella's empty dining room at the opening is a vase standing in the heart of the house 'holding the still, distilled essence of emptiness, silence' (*BA*, 34). Keats's 'Cold Pastoral' may in fact describe the world not only of Isabella's house but that of *Between the Acts*. The final scene is a raised curtain showing an ancestral home that no longer shelters. It is the Oliver family's Pointz Hall, an age-old site now deconstructed and barren – as are the voices heard 'without bodies', and words of one syllable which sink 'down in the mud' (*BA*, 135, 191). Language, history and England have come apart, or stopped, as they would soon stop for Woolf, as this prescient passage suggests:

> The church bells always stopped, leaving you to ask: Won't there be another note? Isa, half-way across the lawn, listened . . . Ding, dong, ding . . . There was not going to be another note. (*BA*, 186)

While at Monk's House in September 1940, 37 Mecklenburgh Square was bombed and their house was badly damaged. No. 52 Tavistock Square was severely hit on 18 October 1940; later visiting the site, Woolf saw it in ruins, commenting on a single surviving wall of her study (*D*, v, 331). On another visit, she wrote that even travelling by bus was impossible: 'streets were being blown up. So by Tube to the Temple; & there wandered in the desolate ruins of my old squares: gashed; dismantled; the old red bricks all white powder' (*D*, v, 353). Later that month, John Lehmann supervised the move of the Hogarth Press from Mecklenburgh Square to Letchworth and in December, the move of Woolf's furniture and books from London to Rodmell for storage at Monk's House and in the village. Increasingly, Woolf was starting to feel that 'we live without a future' (*D*, v, 353).

When Woolf committed suicide, she and Leonard were living full-time at Monk's House but with constant anxiety. Leonard considered joining the Home Guard, while Woolf declared that

'thinking is my fighting' (*D*, V, 285). Even in Sussex enemy planes
flew low overhead and occasionally fired on the countryside.
Invasion seemed imminent and both feared arrest – Leonard,
of course, because he was Jewish. They thought they were on the
Gestapo's 'Black List' – an arrest manifest – which it was later
revealed they were. They made plans for suicide (*D*, V, 284–5).

Mrs Dalloway, preceded by *Jacob's Room* and succeeded by
To the Lighthouse, addressed the war, sometimes obliquely and
sometimes, as with the condition of Septimus Warren Smith,
directly. But in all three works, death on the battlefield was never
heroic. War, as Woolf emphasized in *Three Guineas*, was never a
noble enterprise. The scene of sixteen-year-old recruits marching
towards Whitehall and exhibiting discipline mixed with immaturity
and uncertainty, witnessed by Mrs Dalloway, underscores the
indifference of war to life (*MD*, 43–4).

Woolf experienced increasing despair during this time until it
was unbearable. Headaches, sleeplessness, anxiety and the failure to
concentrate marked its onslaught. She doubted the value of *Between
the Acts* and wrote to John Lehmann, former manager and now
partner at the Hogarth Press, suggesting it not be published. In
the days following, she refused to rest and ate little. Leonard wrote
that 'her thoughts raced beyond her control; she was terrified of
madness.'[22] Octavia Wilberforce, her last doctor, remarked in a letter
that she had lost control over words and become overreactive.[23]

On completing *Between the Acts* and its revision, a nervous,
depressed Woolf needed a new project and, instead of a collection
of more critical essays to be titled 'Reading at Random', hit upon
making a 'living portrait', or picture in words of one of her friends.
Her first thought was Octavia Wilberforce, who had become
another and likely her final female friend. Woolf had already
sketched out Octavia's early childhood in a country house named
Lavington. At first objecting, Octavia then agreed, thinking it would
be a chance for her, with her 'unanalytical mind . . . to talk to a born

Bust of Virginia Woolf in the garden at Monk's House, East Sussex.

clarifier'.[24] Octavia's practical nature stood in contrast to Woolf's constant but debilitating self-analysis. As Woolf herself understood, 'occupation is essential', although she was too enervated to formally begin Octavia's 'portrait', their meeting only a chance for Woolf to tell Octavia about the effect of the imprisoning grief of her father after the death of her mother and the great emotional claims he made upon her and her sister (*D*, v, 358). 'I never remember any enjoyment of my body', she confided to Octavia.[25]

On 28 March, after a visit the day before to Octavia in Brighton, Woolf left Monk's House, leaving two letters on a table in an upstairs sitting room, one for Vanessa, one for Leonard.[26] A third letter, probably written on 18 March and hastily composed to Leonard, lay on her desk in her writing studio in the garden. The letter to Vanessa appears to have been written on 23 March; the one to Leonard shortly after. Both were held in reserve. The note addressed to Vanessa concludes with,

I can hardly think clearly anymore. If I could I would tell
you what you and the children have meant to me. I think
you know, I have fought against it, but I can't any longer.

The letter to Leonard, dated 18 March 1941, begins:

I feel certain that I am going mad again: I feel we can't go
through another of those terrible times. And I shant recover
this time . . . so I am doing what seems the best thing to do. You
have given me the greatest possible happiness . . . I don't think
two people could have been happier till this terrible disease
came . . . I owe all the happiness of my life to you . . . everything
has gone from me but the certainty of your goodness.[27]

The second letter, likely dated 28 March 1941, begins again
with how Leonard has given her 'complete happiness' but also her
awareness that she will never get over her condition. 'All I want to
say', she writes, is that 'until this disease came on we were perfectly
happy, it was all due to you.' It ends with 'will you destroy all my
papers[?]'[28]

At midday, Woolf walked half a mile to the river Ouse and thrust
a large stone into the pocket of her fur coat. She knew how to swim
but threw herself into the river, forcing herself to drown. Discovering
her note, Leonard rushed to the riverbank and located her walking
stick floating in the water, but despite frantic searching her body
would not be recovered for approximately three weeks. Several
teenage cyclists found it on 18 April 1941, a short way downstream
in the river, originally thought to be a floating log. An inquest was
held the next day and the verdict was 'suicide with the balance of
her mind disturbed'. Before the body was discovered, Vita believed
that not finding Woolf's body would be better, hoping that since
'the river is tidal . . . she has probably been carried out to sea. She
loved the sea.'[29]

Lytton Strachey and Virginia Woolf smoking in the garden at Garsington, 1923.

Octavia, in consultation with Leonard before the discovery of Woolf's body, believed that the war might have revived her fears of having another breakdown, such as the one she experienced before and during the First World War. After Octavia left, Leonard wrote a note (undated) admitting that 'I know that she is drowned & yet I listen for her to come in at the door. I know that it is the last page & yet I turn it over.'[30] From the outset, from her early curiosity about the sinking of the *Titanic*, Woolf, the sea and death were interwoven. Instead of the lyrical sense of sinking down into the depths and falling dreamlike to the bottom, she knew that such action did not happen with ease. One had to put stones in one's pockets. She did.

Virginia Woolf was cremated on 21 April with only Leonard present. Her ashes were buried under a great elm tree just outside the garden at the rear of Monk's House, one of two named by the Woolfs 'Leonard and Virginia'. Her epitaph was the concluding words of *The Waves*: 'Against you I will fling myself, unvanquished and unyielding, O Death!'

Virginia Woolf's final words were: 'Will you destroy all my papers'. Written in the margin of her suicide letter to Leonard, it is unclear what 'papers' he was to destroy – the typescript of her last novel *Between the Acts*; the first chapter of *Anon*, a project on the history of English literature; or her prolific diaries and letters? If Woolf wished for all of these papers to be destroyed, Leonard disobeyed. He published her novel, compiled significant diary entries into the volume *The Writer's Diary* and carefully kept all of her manuscripts, diaries and letters, thereby preserving Woolf's unique voice and personality captured in each line. Leonard continued to direct the Hogarth Press until he sold the company to Chatto & Windus in 1946 and lived at Monk's House until his death in 1969.

Epilogue

I shall pass like a cloud on the waves.

Virginia Woolf (*D*, III, 218)

Those who knew Woolf were frequently asked if she was a gloomy or a melancholy individual. Elizabeth Bowen was one. She admitted that in Woolf's presence,

> one could not but be aware, of an undertow often of sadness, of melancholy, of greater fear. But the main impression was of a creature of laughter and movement . . . and her power of conveying enjoyment was extraordinary.

Her laugh, Bowen remembered, was 'in a consuming, choking, delightful, hooting way. And *that* is what has remained with me.' Angelica Garnett remembered that Woolf was,

> never placid, never quite at rest. Even when, knees angular under the lamp and cigarette holder, she sat with a friend after tea, she quivered with interest in the doings of other people.[1]

And of the Bloomsbury Group? No final summing up can be offered, partly because the multitudinous assembly ran for nearly two decades, sharing loves, friendships and death. Rebecca West offered an ironic if uncharitable summary, referring to *À la recherche du temps perdu* when she said Bloomsbury was a

> group who resembled Madame Verdurin's clan but who thought
> they were the Guermantes; and what was fascinating was that
> they had all read Proust, they had seen their own situation
> analyzed to the last trace element and did not recognize it.[2]

The disparity jars but it is not inaccurate. The Verdurins were in the vanguard, attracting the avant-garde and up-and-coming artists; the Guermantes the famous and well established. But at the centre was not Madame Verdurin – it was Virginia Woolf, who would ironically not find herself at home with very few characters from Proust. For West, Woolf seemed at times more of a phantom than a presence.

Virginia Woolf published her earliest works anonymously but when she died she was perhaps the best-known woman novelist in the English-speaking world. In her public life, she seemed to display her genius, while in private she hid her mental despair. As she said of Jane Carlyle, 'few people, indeed, have been able to cast so brilliant an image of themselves upon paper' yet leave their personal life so self-enclosed.[3] Her reputation and reception was worldwide, despite its ups and downs. As she once wrote, 'I am rooted, but I flow', reminding herself and her readers that 'every day I unbury – I dig up. I find relics of myself in the sand' (*w*, 83, 104).

References

Introduction

1 Virginia Woolf, 'Reminiscences', in *Moments of Being*, ed. Jeanne Schulkind, 2nd edn (San Diego, CA, 1985), p. 29.

2 Virginia Woolf, 'A Terrible Tragedy in a Duckpond [with A Note of Correction]', in *A Cézanne in the Hedge and other Memories of Charleston and Bloomsbury*, ed. Hugh Lee (London, 1992), p. 183.

3 John Wilson Foster, *The Titanic Complex: A Cultural Manifest* (Vancouver, 1997), p. 52.

4 Virginia Woolf, 'How Should One Read a Book?' [1926], in *The Common Reader: First and Second Series* (New York, 1948), p. 293.

5 Virginia Woolf, 'Great Men's Houses', in *The London Scene: Six Essays on London Life* (New York, 1975), pp. 31–9 (p. 31).

6 Virginia Woolf, 'Mr Kipling's Notebook' [1920], in *The Essays of Virginia Woolf*, vol. III, ed. Andrew McNeillie (New York, 1988), p. 239.

7 Kate Chopin, *The Awakening*, ed. Margaret Culley (New York, 1976), pp. 113, 114. Like Woolf, Chopin's mentors and friends were mainly women.

8 Virginia Woolf, 'The Serpentine' [1903], in *A Passionate Apprentice: The Early Journals, 1897–1909*, ed. Mitchell A. Leaska (Toronto, 1990), p. 213.

9 Virginia Woolf, 'A Sketch of the Past', in *Moments of Being*, p. 98.

10 Virginia Woolf, 'Literary Geography', in *The Essays of Virginia Woolf*, vol. I, ed. Andrew McNeillie (New York, 1986), p. 35.

11 Virginia Woolf, 'Stopford Brooke', originally published 29 November 1917 in the *TLS*, in *Essays of Virginia Woolf*, vol. II, p. 184. But as she wrote in *Orlando*, 'the true length of a person's life . . . is always a

matter of dispute', a critique partly aimed by her at the rigid structure of the *Dictionary of National Biography*, founded by her father (*or*, 291).

1 22 Hyde Park Gate, 1882–1904

1 Virgina Woolf, 'A Sketch of the Past', in *Moments of Being*, ed. Jeanne Schulkind, 2nd edn (San Diego, CA, 1985), pp. 129–30; Alison Light, *Mrs Woolf and the Servants* (New York, 2008), pp. 31–4.

2 Emma Sutton, *Virginia Woolf and Classical Music: Politics, Aesthetics, Form* (Edinburgh, 2013), p. 18.

3 Woolf, 'A Sketch of the Past', pp. 24, 65.

4 Virginia Woolf, 'Reminiscences', in *Moments of Being*, p. 28.

5 Woolf, 'A Sketch of the Past', pp. 80, 81, 83.

6 Ibid., p. 91.

7 Ibid., pp. 94, 95.

8 Ibid., p. 96.

9 Ibid., p. 97.

10 Ibid., p. 99.

11 Ibid., pp. 105, 103.

12 Vanessa Curtis, *Virginia Woolf's Women* (London, 2002), p. 59.

13 A recent study suggests that Woolf outlined her aesthetic not in an Italian diary of 1908 but earlier, in the so-called Warboys diary of 1899 (Warboys was a village in what was then Huntingdonshire where Stephen and his children spent the summer). See Barbara Lounsberry, *Becoming Virginia Woolf: Her Early Diaries and the Diaries She Read* (Gainesville, FL, 2014), p. 2.

14 Virginia Woolf, entry of 4 April 1897, in *A Passionate Apprentice: The Early Journals, 1897–1909*, ed. Mitchell A. Leaska (Toronto, 1990), p. 66.

15 Lounsberry offers a long list of the diarists Woolf studied, ranging from Emerson, Tolstoy and Chekhov to Beatrice Webb and Katherine Mansfield. See Lounsberry, *Becoming Virginia Woolf*, pp. 3–4.

16 Woolf, 'A Sketch of the Past', p. 108.

17 Ibid., pp. 83, 94.

18 Ibid., pp. 106, 114.

19 Ibid., pp. 91, 93.

20 Ibid., p. 93.

21 Ibid., p. 147.

22 Ibid., p. 118.

23 Woolf, entry of 30 January 1905, in *A Passionate Apprentice*, p. 230.

24 Virginia Woolf, 'Old Bloomsbury' [*c*. 1921–2], in *Moments of Being*,
    p. 183.

25 Vanessa Bell, 'Notes on Bloomsbury' [1951], in *Sketches in Pen and Ink*,
    ed. Lia Giachero (London, 1997), p. 97.

26 Curtis, *Virginia Woolf's Women*, pp. 89, 90–91.

27 Woolf, 'A Sketch of the Past', p. 125.

28 Virginia Woolf, *Flush* [1933], ed. Kate Flint (Oxford, 2009), pp, 32, 27.

29 Virginia Woolf, 'On Not Knowing Greek' [1925], in *The Common
    Reader: First and Second Series* (New York, 1948), p. 39.

30 Ibid., p. 43.

31 Ibid., pp. 44–5, 57.

32 Hermione Lee, *Virginia Woolf* (London, 1996), pp. 124–8.

33 Virginia Woolf, '22 Hyde Park Gate' [*c*. 1920], in *Moments of Being*, p. 177.

34 Woolf, 'Old Bloomsbury', p. 182.

35 See Thomas C. Caramagno's *The Flight of the Mind: Virginia Woolf's
    Art and Manic-depressive Illness* (Berkeley, CA, 1992) and Katherine
    Dalsimer, *Virginia Woolf: Becoming a Writer* (New Haven, CT, 2001).

36 Woolf, 'A Sketch of the Past', p. 151.

37 G. E. Moore, *Principia Ethica* [1903] (Cambridge, 1956), p. 189.

38 Gilles Deleuze, *Foucault*, trans. Seán Hand (Minneapolis, MN, 1988),
    p. 137.

39 Virginia Woolf, *On Being Ill* [1926], intro. Hermione Lee (Ashfield, MA,
    2002), p. 28.

40 Woolf, 'Reminiscences', p. 36.

41 Vita Sackville-West, in *The Letters of Vita Sackville-West to Virginia
    Woolf*, ed. Louise DeSalvo and Mitchell A. Leaska (New York, 1985),
    p. 176.

42 G. Lowes Dickinson, *The Greek View of Life* [1896], preface E. M. Forster
    (Ann Arbor, MI, 1960), p. 185.

43 Sigmund Freud, 'Mourning and Melancholia' [1917], in *On Murder,
    Mourning and Melancholia*, trans. Shaun Whiteside, intro. Maud
    Ellmann (London, 2005), pp. 203, 204.

44 Sigmund Freud, *Civilization and Its Discontents* [1930], trans. and ed.
    James Strachey (New York, 1961), pp. 64–5.

45 A novel by Priya Parmar entitled *Vanessa and Her Sister* (New York, 2014) fictionalizes their lives between 1905 and 1912, relying partly on an invented diary by Vanessa. However, actual letters and documents from the two sisters appear in the text.

46 Leon Edel, *Bloomsbury*: *A House of Lions* (Philadelphia, PA, 1979), p. 100.

2 46 Gordon Square, 1904–7

1 Virginia Woolf, 'Old Bloomsbury' [*c.* 1921–2], in *Moments of Being*, ed. Jeanne Schulkind, 2nd edn (San Diego, CA, 1985), p. 185.

2 Ibid., p. 182.

3 Thomas C. Caramagno, *The Flight of the Mind: Virginia Woolf's Art and Manic-depressive Illness* (Berkeley, CA, 1992), p. 11.

4 Ibid., p. 12.

5 Leonard Woolf, *Beginning Again: An Autobiography of the Years 1911–1918* (London, 1964), p. 76.

6 'What is the difference between a camera and the whooping cough? One makes facsimiles and the other makes sick families. What is the difference between a lion and a tea-pot? There is an n in neither.' *Hyde Park Gate News*, 1/9 (6 April 1891), p. 4.

7 *Hyde Park Gate News: The Stephen Family Newspaper*, ed. Gill Lowe, foreword Hermione Lee (London, 2006), p. 20.

8 Ibid., p. 175.

9 Ibid., pp. 179–80.

10 Leila Brosnan, *Reading Virginia Woolf's Essays and Journalism: Breaking the Surface of Silence* (Edinburgh, 1997), p. 19.

11 Rebecca West, 'Recollection', in *Recollections of Virginia Woolf by her Contemporaries*, ed. Joan Russell Noble (London, 1972).

12 Examples of friends and associates as editors include T. S. Eliot, editor of the *Criterion*, Desmond MacCarthy, editor of the *New Statesman* and later senior literary critic at the *Sunday Times*, John Middleton Murry at the *Athenaeum* and David Garnett, literary editor of the *New Statesman*. For a summary of Woolf's journalism of the 1920s, see Brosnan, *Reading Virginia Woolf's Essays and Journalism*, pp. 50–52.

13 Virginia Woolf, *The Essays of Virginia Woolf*, vol. I, ed. Andrew McNeillie (New York, 1986), p. 23.

14 Frances Spalding, *The Bloomsbury Group*, 2nd edn (London, 2013), p. 67.
15 See Jan Ondaatje Rolls, *The Bloomsbury Cookbook: Recipes for Life, Love and Art* (London, 2014).
16 Vanessa Bell, 'Notes on Bloomsbury' [1951], in *Sketches in Pen and Ink*, ed. Lia Giachero (London, 1997), p. 106.
17 Ibid., pp. 105, 103, 104. Lytton Strachey offered a different, semi-comic impression. Reporting to Leonard Woolf about an early visit to 22 Hyde Park Gate, before Leslie Stephen died, he noted that Virginia 'is rather wonderful, quite witty, full of things to say, and absolutely out of rapport with reality' – in Hermione Lee, *Virginia Woolf* (London, 1996), p. 209.
18 Hermione Lee, 'Virginia Woolf's Essays', in *The Cambridge Companion to Virginia Woolf*, ed. Sue Roe and Susan Sellers (Cambridge, 2000), p. 92.
19 Brosnan, *Reading Virginia Woolf's Essays and Journalism*, p. 62.
20 Virginia Woolf, 'Reviewing', in *The Captain's Death Bed and Other Essays* (London, 1950), p. 121.
21 Woolf, 'Old Bloomsbury', p. 194.
22 Ibid., pp. 195–6.
23 For the implications of such attitudes, see Jessica Berman, 'Woolf and the Private Sphere', in *Virginia Woolf in Context*, ed. Bryony Randall and Jane Goldman (Cambridge, 2012), pp. 461–74.
24 Woolf, 'Old Bloomsbury', pp. 184–5.
25 Vanessa Curtis, *Virginia Woolf's Women* (London, 2002), p. 184.
26 William Plomer, *Autobiography* (London, 1975), p. 334.
27 On the dynamics of the conscientious objectors and social life at Garsington and Morrell's direction of the programme and its consequences, see Victor Luftig, *Seeing Together: Friendship between the Sexes in English Writing from Mill to Woolf* (Stanford, CA, 1993), pp. 169–76.
28 Lady Ottoline Morrell, 'Artists Revels', in *The Bloomsbury Group: A Collection of Memoirs, Commentary and Criticism*, ed. S. P. Rosenbaum (Toronto, 1975), p. 245.
29 Spalding, *The Bloomsbury Group*, pp. 79, 81.
30 Leonard Woolf, *Beginning Again*, p. 198.
31 Virginia Woolf, 'Oxford Street Tide' [January 1932], in *Selected Essays*, ed. David Bradshaw (Oxford, 2008), p. 199.
32 Virginia Woolf, *The London Scene: Six Essays on London Life*, intro. Francine Prose (New York, 1975), p. 76.

33 Virginia Woolf, 'Street Haunting: A London Adventure', in *Selected Essays*, pp. 177, 178.

3 29 Fitzroy Square, 1907–11

 1 Woolf would present a satirical image of George Frederic Watts in her comic play *Freshwater*.
 2 Duncan Grant, 'Virginia Woolf', in *Recollections of Virginia Woolf by her Contemporaries*, ed. Joan Russell Noble (London, 1972), p. 20.
 3 Ibid., pp. 21, 22.
 4 Ibid., pp. 21–2.
 5 Elizabeth Bowen, 'Recollections', in *Recollections of Virginia Woolf*, p. 50; Angelica Garnett, 'Recollections', ibid., p. 84.
 6 Rosamond Lehmann, 'Recollections', ibid., p. 63; David Garnett, 'Recollections', ibid., pp. 108–9.
 7 Virginia Woolf, 'Old Bloomsbury' [*c*. 1921–2], in *Moments of Being*, ed. Jeanne Schulkind, 2nd edn (San Diego, CA, 1985), p. 197.
 8 Virginia Woolf, *Roger Fry: A Biography* (London, 1940), p. 55.
 9 Roger Fry in Virginia Woolf, *Roger Fry* (New York, 1940), p. 183.
10 For Bell on Woolf, see Mark Hussey, *Virginia Woolf A to Z* (New York, 1995), p. 17. A popular quip about Bloomsbury was that 'they lived in squares and loved in triangles.' Ralph Partridge, during his stay with Lytton Strachey and Dora Carrington at Ham Spray, created a recipe for 'Ham Spray Triangles' (ham and cod's roe on toast). It is not clear, however, if he married Carrington before or after he invented the recipe. See Jan Ondaatje Rolls, *The Bloomsbury Cookbook: Recipes for Life, Love and Art* (London, 2014). pp. 160–61; 'love in triangles' remark cited in Nick Rankin, 'Leonard Woolf's Forgotten Sri Lankan Novel', *BBC Magazine* (12 May 2014).
11 Louise DeSalvo, 'Introduction', in Virginia Woolf, *Melymbrosia*, ed. Louise DeSalvo (San Francisco, CA, 2002), p. xx.
12 See ibid., pp. xxii–xxiv. Also DeSalvo, 'Virginia Woolf's Revisions for the 1920 American and English Editions of *The Voyage Out*', *Bulletin of Research in the Humanities*, 82 (Autumn 1979), pp. 338–66.
13 Woolf, *Melymbrosia*, p. 188.

4 38 Brunswick Square, 1911–15

1 Vanessa Bell, 'Notes on Bloomsbury', in *Sketches in Pen and Ink*, ed. Lia Giachero (London, 1997), p. 110.

2 Compton Mackenzie, *The East Wind of Love* (London, 1937), pp. 7–8.

3 Christopher Ondaatje, *Woolf in Ceylon: An Imperial Journey in the Shadow of Leonard Woolf, 1904–1911* (Toronto, 2005), p. xi.

4 Leonard Woolf, *Growing: An Autobiography of the Years 1904–1911* (London, 1961), p. 25.

5 Victoria Glendinning, *Leonard Woolf: A Biography* (New York, 2006), p. 19.

6 Vanessa Bell, *Selected Letters of Vanessa Bell*, ed. Regina Marler (New York, 1993), p. 113.

7 The exchange of letters with the government and the resignation letter appear at the end of his autobiography *Growing*. See also Glendinning, *Leonard Woolf*, p. 132.

8 Leonard Woolf, *Beginning Again: An Autobiography of the Years 1911–1918* (London, 1964), p. 100.

9 Leonard Woolf, *The Wise Virgins* (London, 1914), p. 52.

10 Glendinning, *Leonard Woolf*, p. 138.

11 Hermione Lee, *Virginia Woolf* (London, 1996), p. 307.

12 Leonard Woolf, *Beginning Again*, p. 84.

13 Ibid., p. 54; Lee, *Virginia Woolf*, pp. 325–6.

14 Leonard Woolf, *Beginning Again*, p. 93; Lee, *Virginia Woolf*, p. 326.

15 Leonard Woolf, *The Letters of Leonard Woolf*, ed. Frederic Spotts (San Diego, CA, 1989), p. 188.

16 Jan Ondaatje Rolls, *The Bloomsbury Cookbook: Recipes for Life, Love and Art* (London, 2014), p. 97.

17 Leonard Woolf, *Beginning Again*, p. 168.

18 On the manic and depressive states of Woolf, see Leonard Woolf, *Beginning Again*, pp. 76–7, 161. On the sleeping pill incident, see pp. 156–7. He also gives a useful summary of her mental state on pp. 160–61. See also Nigel Nicolson, *Virginia Woolf* (New York, 2000), p. 55.

19 On the topic of Woolf, food and eating, see Alice Lowe, '"A Certain Hold on Haddock and Sausage": Dining Well in Virginia Woolf's Life and Work', in *Virginia Woolf and the Natural World: Selected Papers of the*

Twentieth Annual International Conference on Virginia Woolf, ed. Kristin Czarnecki and Carrie Rohman (Clemson, SC, 2011), pp. 157–62.

20 Lee, *Virginia Woolf*, p. 178; Leonard Woolf, *Beginning Again*, p. 78.

21 Leonard Woolf quoted in Nicholson, *Virginia Woolf*, p. 56

22 Leonard Woolf, *Beginning Again*, pp. 81, 163.

23 Virginia Woolf, *The Essays of Virginia Woolf*, vol. I, ed. Andrew McNeillie (New York, 1986), p. 28.

24 Robin Majumdar and Allen McLaurin, 'Introduction', in *Virginia Woolf: The Critical Heritage*, ed. Robin Majumdar and Allen McLaurin (London, 1975), p. 5; Lytton Strachey, 'On the Voyage Out', ibid., p. 64.

25 'The Voyage Out', *Times Literary Supplement* (1 April 1915); *Virginia Woolf: The Critical Heritage*, p. 49; *Athenaeum* (1 May 1915), in *Virginia Woolf: The Critical Heritage*, p. 59.

26 Leonard Woolf, *Beginning Again*, pp. 172–3.

27 Ibid., p. 173.

28 Lee, *Virginia Woolf*, p. 279.

29 Ibid., p. 281; Woolf, 'Three Guineas', in *A Room of One's Own and Three Guineas*, ed. Morag Shiach (Oxford, 1998), p. 387.

5 Hogarth House, 34 Paradise Road, Richmond, 1915–24

1 Harold Child, 'Kew Gardens', *Times Literary Supplement* (29 May 1919); *Virginia Woolf: The Critical Heritage*, ed. Robin Majumdar and Allen McLaurin (London, 1975), p. 67.

2 Robert Skidelsky, 'A Tale of Two Houses', in *A Cézanne in the Hedge and Other Memories of Charleston and Bloomsbury*, ed. Hugh Lee (London, 1992), p. 142.

3 Quentin Bell, 'A Cézanne in the Hedge', ibid., pp. 137–8.

4 Ibid., p. 139.

5 Katherine Mansfield, 'Night and Day', *Athenaeum* (21 November 1919); *Virginia Woolf: The Critical Heritage*, p. 80.

6 Helen Wussow, 'Conflict of Language in Virginia Woolf's *Night and Day*', *Journal of Modern Literature*, XVI/1 (1989), p. 62.

7 Leonard Woolf, *Beginning Again: An Autobiography of the Years 1911–1918* (London, 1964), pp. 203, 204.

8 Ibid., p. 204.

9   Nadine Gordimer, 'Introduction', in *Selected Stories* (London, 1975), p. 11.

10 Virginia Woolf, 'My Dear Katherine', 13 February 1921, Smith College Mortimer Rare Book Room, www.smith.edu.

11 n.a., 'Dissolving Views', *Yorkshire Post* (29 November 1922), in *Virginia Woolf: The Critical Heritage*, p. 107.

12 Ezra Pound, 'The Chinese Written Character as a Medium for Poetry', in *Early Writings: Poems and Prose*, ed. Ira B. Nadel (New York, 2005), p. 320.

13 Virginia Woolf, 'A Sketch of the Past', in *Moments of Being: Unpublished Autobiographical Writings*, ed. Jeanne Schulkind (Sussex, 1976), pp. 126–7. This text differs from the 2nd edn of 1985, which reads 'Explorers and revolutionists, as we both were by nature . . .'.

14 'Unconventional Novel, *Jacob's Room*', *The Guardian* (3 November 1922); Rebecca West, 'Jacob's Room', *New Statesman* (4 November 1922), in *Virginia Woolf: The Critical Heritage*, p. 101.

15 Leonard Woolf, *Beginning Again*, p. 232.

16 Ibid., p. 148.

17 Leonard Woolf, *Downhill All the Way: An Autobiography of the Years 1919–1939* (London, 1967), p. 76.

18 Nigel Nicolson, *Portrait of a Marriage* (London, 1973), p. 37. Cf. 34.

19 J. H. Willis, *Leonard and Virginia Woolf as Publishers: The Hogarth Press, 1917–1941* (Charlottesville, VA, 1992), p. 105.

20 Vita Sackville-West, in Nicolson, *Portrait of a Marriage*, p. 200.

21 Vita Sackville-West, in *The Letters of Vita Sackville-West to Virginia Woolf*, ed. Louise DeSalvo and Mitchell A. Leaska (New York, 1985), p. 53.

22 Ibid., p. 238.

23 Ibid., p. 27.

24 Ibid., p. 89.

25 Ibid., p. 165.

6   52 Tavistock Square, 1924–39

1   Nigel Nicolson, *Virginia Woolf* (New York, 2000), p. 101.

2   Jean Moorcroft Wilson, *Virginia Woolf's London: A Guide to Bloomsbury and Beyond* (London, 2000), pp. 107–8.

3   Quentin Bell, *Virginia Woolf*, vol. II (London, 1972), p. 102.

4 Virginia Woolf, 'Modern Fiction', in *Selected Essays*, ed. David
   Bradshaw (Oxford, 2009), pp. 7, 8, 9.
5 Arnold Bennett, 'Is the Novel Decaying?', in *Virginia Woolf: The Critical
   Heritage*, ed. Robin Majumdar and Allen McLaurin (London, 1975),
   p. 113.
6 Virginia Woolf, 'Mr Bennett and Mrs Brown' (first version), in *Virginia
   Woolf: The Critical Heritage*, p. 117. Woolf's review of Dostoevsky's *An
   Honest Thief and Other Stories*, 'Dostoevsky in Cranford', appeared in
   the *Times Literary Supplement* on 23 October 1919.
7 Woolf, 'Mr Bennett and Mrs Brown', p. 119.
8 Virginia Woolf, 'Character in Fiction' [1924], in *Selected Essays*,
   pp. 37, 38.
9 Ibid., p. 44.
10 Ibid., pp. 45, 49.
11 Ibid., pp. 51, 54.
12 Edward Bishop, *A Virginia Woolf Chronology* (Boston, MA, 1989), p. 87.
13 Woolf, 'Character in Fiction', p. 37.
14 Leonard Woolf, *Beginning Again: An Autobiography of the Years 1911–1918*
   (London, 1964), p. 164.
15 Virginia Woolf, 'A Sketch of the Past', in *Moments of Being*, ed. Jeanne
   Schulkind, 2nd edn (San Diego, CA, 1985), p. 69.
16 Ibid., p. 81.
17 Ibid.
18 Roger Fry, *Vision and Design* (London, 1925), p. 239.
19 J. H. Willis, Jr, *Leonard and Virginia Woolf as Publishers: The Hogarth
   Press, 1917–41* (Charlottesville, VA, 1992), p. 132.
20 Arnold Bennett, 'To the Lighthouse', *Evening Standard* (23 June 1927),
   in *Virginia Woolf: The Critical Heritage*, pp. 200–201.
21 Conrad Aiken, 'The Novel as Work of Art', *Dial* (July 1927), in *Virginia
   Woolf: The Critical Heritage*, pp. 207–8.
22 Vita Sackville-West, in *The Letters of Vita Sackville-West to Virginia Woolf*,
   ed. Louise DeSalvo and Mitchell A. Leaska (New York, 1985), p. 238.
23 Ibid., p. 237.
24 Review of *Orlando* in the *Daily Chronicle*, cited in Victoria Glendinning,
   Leonard Woolf: A Biography (New York, 2006), p. 205.
25 J. H. Willis, *Leonard and Virginia Woolf as Publishers: The Hogarth Press,
   1917–1941* (Charlottesville, VA, 1992), p. 133.

26 'Women and Books', *Times Literary Supplement* (24 October 1929), in *Virginia Woolf: The Critical Heritage*, p. 255; Vita Sackville-West, 'Room of One's Own', *Listener* (6 November 1929), ibid., p. 258; Rebecca West, 'Autumn and Virginia Woolf', in *Ending in Earnest: A Literary Log* (Garden City, NY, 1931), p. 211.

27 E. M. Forster, *Virginia Woolf* (Cambridge, 1942), pp. 13–14.

28 Virginia Woolf, 'The Narrow Bridge of Art' [1927], in *Virginia Woolf on Fiction* (London, 2011), p. 19.

29 The author was Frances Cornford, whose *Poems* appeared in 1910. In this section of *Roger Fry* Woolf also writes that Fry had found a plethora of contaminating adjectives and metaphors in literature and that since Cézanne and Picasso had shown the way in art, writers should now 'fling representation to the winds and follow suit'. Virginia Woolf, *Roger Fry: A Biography* (London, 1940), p. 172.

30 Hermione Lee, *Virginia Woolf* (London, 1996), pp. 678–9.

31 Robin Majumdar and Allen McLaurin, 'Introduction', in *Virginia Woolf: The Critical Heritage*, p. 5.

32 Leonard Woolf, *Downhill All the Way: An Autobiography of the Years 1919–1939* (London, 1967), p. 145.

33 Ibid., p. 146; Alice Wood, *Virginia Woolf's Late Cultural Criticism: The Genesis of 'The Years', 'Three Guineas' and 'Between the Acts'* (London, 2013), p. 10.

34 Leonard Woolf, *Downhill All the Way*, p. 146.

7 Monk's House I, 1919–37

1 Alison Light, *Mrs Woolf and the Servants* (New York, 2008), pp. 143, 171.

2 Leila Brosnan, *Reading Virginia Woolf's Essays and Journalism: Breaking the Surface of Silence* (Edinburgh, 1997), p. 149.

3 *Moments of Being* (1976, 1985) contains the most important collection of such works: 'Reminiscences', 'A Sketch of the Past' and three contributions to the Memoir Club: '22 Hyde Park Gate', 'Old Bloomsbury' and 'Am I a Snob?'. See *Moments of Being: Unpublished Autobiographical Writings*, ed. Jeanne Schulkind (Sussex, 1976) and *Moments of Being*, ed. Jeanne Schulkind, 2nd edn (San Diego, CA, 1985).

4 Virginia Woolf, *The Essays of Virginia Woolf*, vol. I, ed. Andrew McNeillie (New York, 1986), p. 249.

5 Peter Monro Jack, 'Virginia Woolf's Richest Novel', *New York Times*, 11 April 1937, available at www.nytimes.com/books

8 Monk's House II, 1938–41

1 Winifred Holtby in Alice Wood, *Virginia Woolf's Late Cultural Criticism: The Genesis of 'The Years', 'Three Guineas' and 'Between the Acts'* (London, 2013), p. 10.

2 See ibid., pp. 10, 2.

3 Q. D. Leavis, 'Caterpillars of the Commonwealth Unite!', *Scrutiny* (September 1938), p. 204. The full review is on pp. 203–14. Later, on p. 208, Leavis complains that Woolf's most 'cherished project of all is to uproot criticism root and branch in the Nazi manner'. Towards the end of her review, she suggests that Woolf should be campaigning for co-education and a change in the social structure, which would permit the daughters of any men to enter the highest course of studies they are fitted for (p. 213). The tone of the book is deplorable, she also adds.

4 Ibid., pp. 204, 210.

5 Commentary on the five photographs is extensive, Elena Gualtieri making the point that the content, style and composition of the published images closely resembles those of similar illustrations found in Woolf's scrapbooks, which she compiled between 1931 and 1937 in preparation for writing *Three Guineas*. See Gualtieri, '*Three Guineas* and the Photograph: The Art of Propaganda', in *Women Writers of the 1930s: Gender, Politics and History*, ed. Maroula Joannou (Edinburgh, 1999), p. 166.

6 Vita Sackville-West, in *The Letters of Vita Sackville-West to Virginia Woolf*, ed. Louise DeSalvo, Mitchell A. Leaska, p. 412.

7 Virginia Woolf, in *The Letters of Vita Sackville-West to Virginia Woolf*, ed. DeSalvo and Leaska (New York, 1985), p. 414.

8 Emily Dalgarno explains (or defends) their absence as Woolf's acknowledgement of both 'Spanish censorship and British cultural conventions by not printing the photographs of the dead to which she refers.' Rather, Woolf plays on the idea of the photograph as a sign of

what is not there. See Dalgarno, *Virginia Woolf and the Visible World* (Cambridge, 2001), p. 157. For a reproduction of the front page of *L'Humanité* for 11 November 1936, with a prominent photo of a dead Spanish child, see p. 163.

9 Ulrich Baer, *Spectral Evidence: The Photography of Trauma* (Cambridge, 2002), p. 9.

10 Ibid., p. 8.

11 Virginia Woolf, 'Three Guineas', in *A Room of One's Own and Three Guineas*, ed. Morag Shiach (Oxford, 1998), p. 292.

12 Ibid., p. 363. See also Maggie Humm, 'Cinema and Photography', in *Virginia Woolf in Context*, ed. Bryony Randall and Jane Goldman (Cambridge, 2012), pp. 295–6. The essay distils Humm's commentary on Woolf and photography in *Modernist Women and Visual Cultures: Virginia Woolf, Vanessa Bell, Photography and Cinema* (New Brunswick, NJ, 2003). In her essay, Humm claims that photography, 'particularly the mass circulation of Kodaks . . . made arguably, the greatest contribution to the changing visual consciousness of modernity as a whole' (p. 296). Also useful is Humm, *Snapshots of Bloomsbury: Private Lives of Virginia Woolf and Vanessa Bell* (New Brunswick, NJ, 2005).

13 For reproductions, see Mary Ann Caws, *Virginia Woolf* (London, 2001), p. 67.

14 Virginia Woolf, 'A Sketch of the Past', in *Moments of Being*, ed. Jeanne Schulkind, 2nd edn (San Diego, CA, 1985), p. 72.

15 On the topic of Woolf and photography, see Maggie Humm, 'Virginia Woolf's Photography and the Monk's House Albums', in *Virginia Woolf in the Age of Mechanical Reproduction*, ed. Pamela L. Caughie (London, 2013), pp. 219–48.

16 Ethel Smyth, in Vanessa Curtis, *Virginia Woolf's Women* (London, 2002), p. 184.

17 Virginia Woolf, *Diary*, vol. v, p . 248; Leonard Woolf, *Downhill All the Way: An Autobiography of the Years 1919–1939* (London, 1967), pp. 168–9.

18 Virginia Woolf, in *The Letters of Vita Sackville-West to Virginia Woolf*, p. 426.

19 Virginia Woolf, *Roger Fry: A Biography* (London, 1940), p. 269.

20 Woolf, in *The Letters of Vita Sackville-West to Virginia Woolf*, pp. 433, 434.

21 Ibid., p. 435.

22 Leonard Woolf, *The Journey Not the Arrival Matters: An Autobiography of the Years 1939–1969* (New York, 1970), p. 91.

23 Herbert Marder, *The Measure of Life: Virginia Woolf's Last Years* (Ithaca, NY, 2000), p. 351.

24 Woolf quoted in ibid., p. 331.

25 Ibid., p. 333.

26 Hermione Lee, *Virginia Woolf* (London, 1996), p. 760. Marder says they were on a mantelpiece in the living room in *The Measure of Life*, p. 341.

27 Virginia Woolf, in Marder, *The Measure of Life*, pp. 336, 342.

28 Lee, *Virginia Woolf*, p. 760.

29 Vita Sackville-West, in Victoria Glendinning, *Leonard Woolf: A Biography* (New York, 2006), p. 330.

30 Leonard Woolf, in Marder, *The Measure of Life*, p. 343.

Epilogue

1 Elizabeth Bowen, 'Recollections', in *Recollections of Virginia Woolf by Her Contemporaries*, ed. Joan Russell Noble (London, 1972), pp. 49, 50. Angelica Garnett, 'Recollections', ibid., p. 86.

2 Rebecca West, 'Recollections', ibid., p. 89.

3 Virginia Woolf, *The Essays of Virginia Woolf*, vol. 1, ed. Andrew McNeillie (New York, 1986), p. 54.

Select Bibliography

Works

The Voyage Out (1915)
'A Mark on the Wall', *Two Stories* (1917)
'Kew Gardens' (1919)
Night and Day (1919)
Monday or Tuesday (1921)
Jacob's Room (1922)
The Common Reader: First Series (1925)
Mrs Dalloway (1925)
To the Lighthouse (1927)
Orlando: A Biography (1928)
A Room of One's Own (1929)
The Waves (1931)
The Common Reader: Second Series (1932)
Flush: A Biography (1933)
The Years (1937)
Three Guineas (1938)
Roger Fry: A Biography (1940)

Posthumous Works

Between the Acts (1941)
The Death of the Moth and Other Essays, ed. Leonard Woolf (1942)
A Haunted House and Other Short Stories, ed. Leonard Woolf (1943)

The Moment and Other Essays, ed. Leonard Woolf (1947)

The Captain's Death Bed and Other Essays, ed. Leonard Woolf (1950)

A Writer's Diary ed. Leonard Woolf (1953)

Granite and Rainbow, ed. Leonard Woolf (1958)

Essays, in *Contemporary Writers*, ed. Jean Guiguet (1965)

Collected Essays, vols I–IV, ed. Leonard Woolf (1966–7)

A Cockney's Farming Experiences (juvenilia), ed. Suzanne Henig (1972)

Mrs Dalloway's Party (short stories), ed. Stella McNichol (1973)

The Flight of the Mind: Collected Letters, vol. I: *1888–1912*, ed. Nigel Nicolson
    with Joanne Trautmann (1975)

Moments of Being (1976), 2nd edn, ed. Jeanne Schulkind (1985)

Freshwater: A Comedy, ed. Lucio P. Ruotolo (1976)

The Question of Things Happening: Collected Letters, vol. II: *1912–22*,
    ed. Nigel Nicolson with Joanne Trautmann (1976)

The Diary of Virginia Woolf, vol. I: *1915–19*, ed. Anne Olivier Bell (1977)

*Books and Portraits: Some Further Selections from the Literary and
    Biographical Writings of Virginia Woolf*, ed. Mary Lyon (1977)

A Change of Perspective: Collected Letters, vol. III: *1923–8*, ed. Nigel Nicolson
    and Joanne Trautmann (1977)

The Diary of Virginia Woolf, vol. II: *1920–24*, ed. Anne Olivier Bell with
    Andrew McNeillie (1978)

A Reflection of the Other Person: The Letters of Virginia Woolf, vol. IV:
    1929–31, ed. Nigel Nicolson and Joanne Trautmann (1978)

Virginia Woolf: Women and Writing (selected essays), ed. Michele Barrett
    (1979)

The Sickle Side of the Moon, Collected Letters, vol. V: *1932–5*,
    ed. Nigel Nicolson and Joanne Trautmann (1979)

The Diary of Virginia Woolf, vol. III, ed. Anne Olivier Bell
    with Andrew McNeillie (1980)

Leave the Letters Till We're Dead, Collected Letters, vol. VI: *1936–41*,
    ed. Nigel Nicolson with Joanne Trautmann (1980)

The Diary of Virginia Woolf, vol. IV, ed. Anne Olivier Bell
    with Andrew McNeillie (1982)

The Diary of Virginia Woolf, vol. V, ed. Anne Olivier Bell
    with Andrew McNeillie (1984)

The Complete Shorter Fiction of Virginia Woolf, ed. Susan Dick (1985)

The Essays of Virginia Woolf, ed. Andrew McNeillie, 3 vols (1986–8)

Congenial Spirits: The Selected Letters of Virginia Woolf,
  ed. Joanne Trautmann Banks (1989)
A Moment's Liberty: The Shorter Diary of Virginia Woolf,
  ed. Anne Oliver Bell (1990)
A Passionate Apprentice: The Early Journals, 1897–1900,
  ed. Mitchell A. Leaska (1990)
Paper Darts: The Illustrated Letters, ed. Frances Spalding (1991)
A Woman's Essays: Selected Essays, vol. I, ed. Rachel Bowlby (1992)
Selected Short Stories, ed. Sandra Kemp (1993)
The Crowded Dance of Modern Life: Selected Essays, vol. II,
  ed. Rachel Bowlby (1993)
Travels with Virginia Woolf (travel writings), ed. Jan Morris (1993)
The Essays of Virginia Woolf, vol. IV, ed. Andrew McNeillie (1994)
The Essays of Virginia Woolf, vol. V, ed. Stuart N. Clarke (2009)
The Essays of Virginia Woolf, vol. VI, ed. Stuart N. Clarke (2011)

Biographies

Bell, Quentin, *Virginia Woolf: A Biography*, 2 vols (London, 1973)
Caws, Mary Ann, *Women of Bloomsbury: Virginia, Vanessa and Carrington*
  (New York, 1990)
Edel, Leon, *Bloomsbury: A House of Lions* (Philadelphia, PA, 1979)
Forrester, Viviane, *Virginia Woolf*, trans. Jody Gladding (New York, 2015)
Gordon, Lyndall, *Virginia Woolf: A Writer's Life* (Oxford, 1984)
Harris, Alexandra, *Virginia Woolf* (London, 2011)
King, James, *Virginia Woolf* (London, 1994)
Leaska, Mitchell, *Granite and Rainbow: The Hidden Life of Virginia Woolf*
  (New York, 1998)
Lee, Hermione, *Virginia Woolf* (London, 1996)
Marder, Herbert, *The Measure of Life: Virginia Woolf's Last Years*
  (Ithaca, NY, 2000)
Poole, Roger, *The Unknown Virginia Woolf*, 4th edn (Cambridge, 1995)
Rose, Phyllis, *Woman of Letters: A Life of Virginia Woolf*
  (New York, 1978)

Works about Woolf

Anscombe, Isabelle, *Omega and After: Bloomsbury and the Decorative Arts*
　　(London, 1981)
Bell, Quentin, *Bloomsbury* (London, 1986)
Bell, Vanessa, *Selected Letters of Vanessa Bell*, ed. Regina Marler (New York, 1993)
Bennett, Arnold, 'Is the Novel Decaying?', *Cassell's Weekly*
　　(28 March 1923), in *Virginia Woolf: The Critical Heritage*, ed. Robin
　　Majumdar and Allen McLaurin (London, 1975), pp. 112–14
Brosnan, Leila, *Reading Virginia Woolf's Essays and Journalism:*
　　Breaking the Surface of Silence (Edinburgh, 1997)
Caramagno, Thomas C., *The Flight of the Mind: Virginia Woolf's Art and*
　　Manic-depressive Illness (Berkeley, CA, 1992)
Chan, Evelyn Tsz Yan, *Virginia Woolf and the Professions* (Cambridge, 2014)
Curtis, Anthony, *Virginia Woolf: Bloomsbury & Beyond* (London, 2006)
Curtis, Vanessa, *The Hidden Houses of Virginia Woolf and Vanessa Bell*
　　(London, 2005)
——, *Virginia Woolf's Women* (London, 2002)
Dalsimer, Katherine, *Virginia Woolf: Becoming a Writer* (New Haven, CT, 2001)
DeSalvo, Louise, *Virginia Woolf: The Impact of Childhood Sexual Abuse*
　　on her Life and Work (Boston, MA, 1989)
Dubino, Jeanne, ed., *Virginia Woolf and the Literary Marketplace*
　　(New York, 2010)
—— et al., eds, *Virginia Woolf: Twenty-first-century Approaches*
　　(Edinburgh, 2015)
Eaton, John P., and Charles A. Hass, *Titanic: Triumph and Tragedy*,
　　2nd edn (New York, 1995)
Forster, E. M., *Virginia Woolf* (Cambridge, 1942)
Froula, Christine, *Virginia Woolf and the Bloomsbury Avant-garde:*
　　War, Civilization, Modernity (New York, 2005)
Gillespie, Diane F., ed., *The Multiple Muses of Virginia Woolf*
　　(New York, 1993)
Glendinning, Victoria, *Leonard Woolf: A Biography* (New York, 2006)
——, *Vita: The Life of V. Sackville-West* (London, 1983)
Gualtieri, Elena, *Virginia Woolf's Essays: Sketching the Past* (London, 2000)
Hancock, Nuala, *Charleston and Monk's House: The Intimate House Museums*
　　of Virginia Woolf and Vanessa Bell (Edinburgh, 2012)

Humm, Maggie, ed., *Edinburgh Companion to vw and the Arts* (Edinburgh, 2010)

Hussey, Mark, *Virginia Woolf A to Z* (New York, 1995)

Kirkpatrick, B. J., and Stuart N. Clarke, *A Bibliography of Virginia Woolf*,
    4th edn (Oxford, 1997)

Koppen, R. S., *Virginia Woolf, Fashion and Literary Modernity*
    (Edinburgh, 2011)

Laurence, Patricia, *Lily Briscoe's Chinese Eyes: Bloomsbury, Modernism and
    China* (Columbia, SC, 2003)

Lehmann, John, *Thrown to the Woolfs: Leonard and Virginia Woolf
    and the Hogarth Press* (New York, 1978)

Lounsberry, Barbara, *Becoming Virginia Woolf: Her Early Diaries
    and the Diaries She Read* (Gainesville, FL, 2014)

Love, Jean O., *Virginia Woolf: Sources of Madness and Art*
    (Berkeley, CA, 1977)

Marcus, Jane, ed., *Virginia Woolf and Bloomsbury: A Centenary Celebration*
    (London, 1987)

——, *Virginia Woolf and The Languages of Patriarchy*
    (Bloomington, IN, 1987)

Marcus, Laura, *Virginia Woolf: Writers and their Work*, 2nd edn (Devon, 2004)

Nicolson, Nigel, *Portrait of a Marriage: Vita Sackville-West and Harold
    Nicolson* (London, 1973)

Noble, Joan Russell, ed., *Recollections of Virginia Woolf by Her Contemporaries*
    (New York, 1972)

Oldfield, Sybil, ed., *Afterwords: Letters on the Death of Virginia Woolf*
    (New Brunswick, NJ, 2005)

Philips, Kathy J., *Virginia Woolf against Empire* (Knoxville, TN, 1994)

Raitt, Suzanne, *Vita and Virginia: The Work and Friendship of V. Sackville-West
    and Virginia Woolf* (Oxford, 1993)

Randall, Bryony, and Jane Goldman, eds, *Virginia Woolf in Context*
    (Cambridge, 2012)

Reed, Christopher, *Bloomsbury Rooms: Modernism, Subculture,
    and Domesticity* (New Haven, CT, 2004)

Reinhold, Natalya, ed., *Woolf Across Cultures* (New York, 2004)

Rolls, Jan Ondaatje, *The Bloomsbury Cookbook: Recipes for Life, Love and Art*
    (London, 2014)

Rosenbaum, S. P., ed., *The Bloomsbury Group: A Collection of Memoirs,
    Commentary and Criticism* (Toronto, 1975)

Rosner, Victoria, ed., *The Cambridge Companion to the Bloomsbury Group* (Cambridge, 2014)

Sackville-West, Vita, *The Letters of Vita Sackville-West to Virginia Woolf*, ed. Louise DeSalvo and Mitchell A. Leaska (New York, 1985)

Sellers, Susan, ed., *The Cambridge Companion to Virginia Woolf* (Cambridge, 2010)

Shone, Richard, *The Art of Bloomsbury: Roger Fry, Vanessa Bell and Duncan Grant*, with essays by James Beechey and Richard Morphet (Princeton, NJ, 1999)

——, *Bloomsbury Portraits: Vanessa Bell, Duncan Grant and their Circle* (Oxford, 1976)

Silver, Brenda R., *Virginia Woolf Icon* (Chicago, IL, 1999)

——, *Virginia Woolf's Reading Notebooks* (Princeton, NJ, 1983)

Smith, Angela, *Katherine Mansfield and Virginia Woolf: A Public of Two* (Oxford, 1999)

Spalding, Frances, *The Bloomsbury Group*, 2nd edn (London, 2013)

——, *Virginia Woolf: Art, Life and Vision* (London, 2014)

Sproles, Karyn Z., *Desiring Women: The Partnership of Virginia Woolf and Vita Sackville-West* (Toronto, 2006)

Stape, J. H., *Virginia Woolf: Interviews and Recollections* (London, 1995)

Sutton, Emma, *Virginia Woolf and Classical Music: Politics, Aesthetics, Form* (Edinburgh, 2013)

Willis, J. H., *Leonard and Virginia Woolf as Publishers: The Hogarth Press, 1917–1941* (Charlottesville, VA, 1992)

Wilson, Duncan, *Leonard Woolf: A Political Biography* (London, 1978)

Wood, Alice, *Virginia Woolf's Late Cultural Criticism: The Genesis of 'The Years', 'Three Guineas' and 'Between the Acts'* (London, 2013)

Woolf, Leonard, *An Autobiography*, intro. Quentin Bell, vol. I: *1880–1911*, vol. II: *1911–69* (Oxford, 1980)

——, *Letters of Leonard Woolf*, ed. Frederic Spotts (San Diego, CA, 1989)

Zwerdling, Alex, *Virginia Woolf and the Real World* (Berkeley, CA, 1986)

Acknowledgements

Among those who helped in my attempt to grasp Virginia Woolf and her world, and to whom I offer thanks, are Helen Wussow, former dean of Continuing Studies at Simon Fraser University, who provided me with the opportunity to discuss *Three Guineas* at the 23rd International Virginia Woolf Conference; Mark Byron of the University of Sydney, who generously invited me to speak on Woolf and Orientalism at a Transnational Modernisms conference in December 2014; and two former colleagues at the University of British Columbia, now retired: John Hulcoop, early enthusiast of Woolf and John X. Cooper, modernist *bon vivant*. Brenda Maddox remains an inspiring biographer filled with energy, wit and the good sense to choose fascinating subjects, while Michael Leaman had the confidence to allow me the opportunity to pursue Woolf from yet another angle. More broadly, the work of numerous Woolf scholars has paved the way for others to follow. I am grateful. But it would be impossible to research and write about Woolf without the alternately comic and thoughtful support of my daughter Dara and son Ryan, while Anne MacKenzie offered continual insight into the psychological make-up of Woolf, Leonard and Vita Sackville-West, read all the relevant texts, joined me in visiting the key sites and kept me from confusions great and small.

Photo Acknowledgements

The author and publishers wish to express their thanks to the following
sources of illustrative material and/or permission to reproduce it.

Photo Alexander Turnbull Library, Wellington, New Zealand
(Ref. MNZ-2532-1/2-F): p. 112; photos © the Charleston Trust:
pp. 19, 104 (photo © Tony Tree on behalf of the Charleston Trust);
photos Houghton Library, Harvard College Library, Cambridge,
Massachusetts (Harvard Theatre Collection): pp. 21, 25, 102, 123, 126,
130, 164, 188; photo Mortimer Rare Book Room, Smith College, Library,
Northampton, Massachusetts (Leslie Stephen Photograph Album):
p. 22; photo Myrabella: p. 60 (this file is licensed under the Creative
Commons Attribution-Share Alike 3.0 Unported license, and any reader
is free to share – to copy, distribute and transmit the work, or to remix –
to adapt the work, under the following conditions – you must attribute
the work in the manner specified by the author or licensor, but not in
any way that suggests that they endorse you or your use of the work);
photos National Portrait Gallery, London: pp. 13, 37, 49, 61, 69, 70,
83, 103, 106, 117, 120, 162, 173; photos © National Trust Photo Library:
pp. 113, 114, 174, 186; photos Ramsey and Muspratt collection, reproduced
courtesy of Peter Lofts: pp. 149, 155; photoSpudgun67: p. 92 (this file is
licensed under the Creative Commons Attribution 2.0 Generic license,
and any reader is free to share – to copy, distribute and transmit the
work, or to remix – to adapt the work, under the following conditions
– you must attribute the work in the manner specified by the author or
licensor, but not in any way that suggests that they endorse you or your
use of the work); photos Tate, London: pp. 11, 52, 84, 105, 107.